T0193432

Heavenly Lessons

Things to Know for the New Age

PAUL BILLINS HENINGTON

authorHOUSE®

AuthorHouse™
1663 Liberty Drive
Bloomington, IN 47403
www.authorhouse.com
Phone: 1 (800) 839-8640

Published by AuthorHouse 05/28/2019

ISBN: 978-1-7283-1344-3 (sc)
ISBN: 978-1-7283-1342-9 (hc)
ISBN: 978-1-7283-1343-6 (e)

Introduction

I have often found myself wondering what amazing and exciting times we live in at this time. It was during my adolescent years which exposed me to the meaning behind these tumultuous events. I call this time when I was out-of-body my time in the intergalactic classroom because I was in a classroom like setting with other individuals from across the planet. Even though my physical body was in bed during these times, I had astrally projected to the classroom every night. I learned that the planet and everything on it goes through periods of change known as Ages. These Ages are represented by astrological signs and have periods of time in between which are called transition periods. We moved into the Aquarian age on March 21st, 1981. What we are experiencing now is transition between the Piscean Age and the Aquarian Age.

The transition has brought many changes such as wars, famine, weather disruptions, planetary destruction, and global warming are common events during this time. Beyond this external chaos, we experience an inner chaos as well. Dramatic changes in life are occurring in many people these days as they clear the way for the new paradigm. This book will strive to Enlighten those that need to bring Order out of the Chaos. Our world is getting smaller with each passing day via the Internet and a global economy. The result is we must learn to cooperate with each other in order to survive.

What is the Intergalactic classroom? It consists of my personal experiences growing up in the classroom. From 12 to 18, I spent my nights astrally projecting and attending a classroom with 24 other individuals from across the planet. We were taught by several ascended masters and other extraterrestrial entities that have walked this planet throughout the ages. This book provides the basic information that was provided the first year and a half of my training in the Intergalactic classroom. The basic theme is we are all human beings striving to find the basics of happiness, love and security. This book will delve into ways in which we can better understand each other in order to end the hypocrisy of hatred and indifference. We are evolving into what it means to be a human being and a human race. Now is the time we can better understand what has left many people confused and uncertain about anything from any source.

We can find the answers we need during this planetary change. We will have to work harder towards understanding and peace.

This book looks at the shifting morality and the daily dilemmas that we all face as we enter into the Aquarian Age. The shifting realities bombard our value systems. Therefore, our choices become more difficult. Sorting out the difference between right and wrong, Good and Evil can only be solved by going within ourselves to find the answers.

The decline of the Patrician religious systems on our planet only exacerbates this dilemma of shifting morality. Their dogmatic approach to morality alienates most people. Thus, many people find themselves guided to deeper spirituality, a sense of self-knowing that is based upon the respect and love for all life on the planet.

In the early chapters of the book, I establish the foundation of deep spiritual training that encourages people to remain solid and grounded in their sense of self. In chapter 1, I discuss what the Aquarian Age means and why the transition is so important. In Chapter 2, I discuss the basics things everyone should know how to do. In Chapter 3 I discuss the psychic aspects and how it relates to your psychic abilities. In Chapter 4, I discuss the seven levels of reincarnation. In Chapter 5, I discuss the social hierarchy and the nine major extraterrestrial races. In Chapter 6, I discuss the eight aspects of love and how it and laughter are so important in this New Age. All Life is a circle and everything thought lost can and will be found again to the betterment of everything on this planet.

This book is for those people that are looking for a better explanation about why the world is going through such dramatic changes. It, also, offers those that are seeking a better way to live their life. It is my wish to share my experiences and visions of the future in a hope that it will trigger others to awaken to a fuller and more Enlightened state.

Love and happiness should be the goal of every individual on this planet. These truths show us that we no longer need to allow those few individuals with extreme greed to dominate our empowerment towards the future. In this time the possibilities are there for all of us to create new realities based on respect and understanding. What are these new realities and how are these concepts of creating new ways of being, We are no longer divided by race or religion, of course, only time will tell as we change.

Humanity's first big hurdle in the process is happening now through terrorism and fear. This book is designed to awaken, prepare, and help you to begin the process. For those who are here to be of service, time is no longer a luxury. We must all awaken to our individual Dharma and do what we are here to do. As the world changes, are we going to change with it or are we going to wallow in the fear that nothing will ever change? The choice is yours! Follow the Heavenly Lessons in your spiritual life to continue on the path. Be Blessed! Be Love! Be Happy!

Acknowledgements

I want to acknowledge the following people that have been on my team to make this book a reality.

Annette Tyo, Suzanne Mitchem, Julie Gliszinski, Juels Yaklin, Kandi Lewis, Corrine Feinberg, Alda Lee, Melda Henry, Evrim Kaya Orucoglu, Barbara Burk, Marie Davis, Cyndi Feilder, Suzzanne Moore, Grace Divine, EJ Smith, Alfredo Oliva, Amy Ponfick, Gina Weisling, Rita French, Moreen DeLong, Sylvia Toenjes Belli, and Erin York thank you for reading my book and helping me to get it out there to the people.

Special Thanks goes to Joumana Massoud for taking your time to edit the transciption from the original manuscript. To Joe Boni and Marion Wallsten for being my rocks and sounding boards. I love you all and I am truly blessed to have you all in my life!

Who I am

To understand my perspective, I should explain my background because my soul journey is closely tied to my family. I was selected to participate in the Intergalactic Classroom before my birth by myself and the Spiritual Hierarchy. My life growing up was fairly ordinary in fact my family wasn't so very odd. We have been reincarnated together as a family for many lifetimes. Albeit, they are not my original family but they are mine and I love them. On both sides of my family there is a strong connection to the spiritual side of life. Therefore, most my family is driven by a desire to serve others.

Here is a short version of my story to help you understand me better. Several billion years ago a star exploded. The star dust created from that explosion helped in my formation. I was born on April 20th 1969 at 9:03 p.m. (my mother still reminds me). The most important people in my young life were my paternal grandmother and great Aunt. They were known as Guardians and they protected various portals to other dimensions. They taught me to sort out the difference between the Unseen and the Seen. For example they taught me the basics of utilizing my gifts to communicate with the deceased. They also helped me by providing a deep connection to the spiritual side of life.

At puberty everything started to coalesce for me. Several things happened that led to my involvement in the Intergalactic classroom. First my next door neighbor died which triggered my latent ability to communicate with the dead. Second, I performed a seance. Finally, Archangel Michael came to me and took me on an astral journey. While I was sleeping one night Archangel Michael came and took me on a tour of the Universe. Together we journeyed to many worlds. We saw nebulae, planets, black holes, binary stars, trinary stars and comets. He took me to see the home worlds of the major alien races like the Sirians and the Pleiadians. I saw cities made of crystal floating in the skies on land and under the seas. They were more advanced than our species and their technology was organic in nature. They existed in harmony with nature. I was truly awestruck! To this day, I do not think I can ever fully describe the full experience to anyone. I do not know how long we traveled or how far because it all seemed to happen outside of space and time.

He told me many things. He said, "You have been chosen because you have a gift needed to accomplish the task ahead and you have done this job many other times in different lifetimes." Furthermore, he said, "You will not be alone. There will be others that share in this service to humanity."

He said, "You will attend a classroom every night for the next six years and you will learn many things that were, are, and will be. You will leave your physical form every night to attend the classroom. When you are done we will serve the Council of Light as Helper and and Guide to those that wish to move closer to God."

He next warned me, "You will be persecuted by some because they do not understand God and the hierarchy of Heaven. Some will love you because they see the light of Love in Your Heart. Hold fast to your faith and trust that all things will be revealed to people when the time is right. Part of your purpose is to share what you have learned in this place and counsel people to become all that they were meant to be."

The last thing we did was to take me by a pink planet in the Pleiadian System. He said to me, "This place is where your soul came from many long years ago. Its name is very long in your original tongue but in English it is pronounced Cha' Chu' Na."

As I looked over the vista of my original home, I felt a sense of homecoming and joy. It had many cities floating in the skies. The air was thick with gases giving it a pinkish glow. I looked and I could see beings flying on wings of Light through the air. I heard singing from all around me and felt great joy filling my heart.

He said, "This is the place where you can always visit and you will return to when you have completed your mission. You have been selected to become a Guardian for the Earth. You are to remain on Earth until you have shared all of your knowledge. You are here to teach the awakened ones how to be good caretakers/stewards of the New Earth. It will help to restore balance on the planet and ensure a thousand years of Peace." Finally he said to me, "I will see you later, little brother."

The next thing I was in my room and had to get ready for regular school. I thought, "Wow! What a neat dream." However, I realized later when I went to sleep again it was more than just a dream. Over the course of the next six years I spent my days in the mundane world while also in the other dimensions. The classroom that the Archangel Michael mentioned was the Intergalactic classroom. It consisted of students from across the planet Earth.

The first year was mainly about learning where we are and where we are going in the bigger picture. We learned about our abilities and how best to utilize them to the betterment of the planet's evolution. We perfected our skills in the second year and learned more about the other species from other planets in the Milky Way galaxy. Through this knowledge, it provided a better understanding and acceptance of each of the other races. In the third year, we were split up into smaller groups to be trained in the more specific nature of our individual service to the planet. With my advanced visionary skills they showed me most of the things that would happen to the to the people of the Earth due to Greed, Lust and Avarice. I was part of a subgroup that consisted of six others from across the planet. We all shared and grew together as the years progressed.

In the fourth and fifth years our duties increased. We were given many tests to see whether we were ready to begin our missions. Those were some of the toughest years for me because I knew what would happen to the people of the Earth. All the pain and suffering took a toll on my burgeoning empathic abilities. I did not believe that I could actually survive living the future I saw and felt it in reality. Unfortunately, the future has not changed and some of the things I saw have already taken place. There are many more things to come. During this time we were assigned a mentor/master to work with us in achieving our specific mission. The Archangel Michael and several other Ascended Masters worked with me to garner a deeper understanding of my mission.

I learned many things during my tutelage. They taught me many forgotten secrets that have been lost for eons. They told me to wait until the time was right to reveal my knowledge to the world. I know now the time has come to share what I learned with the world. Upon my completion of training I was given a seat on the Council of the One. This Council is the highest council that does the bidding of the God Source. After so many years of service, I am an Elder of council and this book is the beginning of fulfilling my mission here on Earth. We are all facing one of the darkest times in human history. This book is designed to help people who are ready to Ascend to the next level and help the planet Ascend as well. Many others have written about some information here as with all things in the New Age.

What is this all about? The Aquarian Age, the Transition Period, and the New Morality.

L ife is always evolving. In fact, history has provided an excellent picture of some of the most interesting changes in our past. Another word for change at this level is critical mass. Critical mass refers to the way the whole of humanity thinks about how things are going to change. When there is a revolution or a major shift in the way people think about things this is a time of critical mass. One of the key things about entering into any new age is a shift in Consciousness about the way things are being done. This paradigm shift in Consciousness is known as the transition period. These times of critical mass usually result in radical Paradigm shifts in the larger reality. Indeed, this is not the first new age or transition. We actually entered into the Age of Pisces about 2,000 years ago, and the the Piscean Age officially ended on, March 20ᵗʰ, 1983. Like any of the other transition periods, between the new and the old ages there is a major time of readjustment. A Transition Period generally lasts about 100 years or fifty years on either side of a specific date of change. Therefore, we have been experiencing major shifts in all of reality since 1933, and it will go up to 2033. Beyond the basic facts about this new age and the transition period, there are symbolic meanings behind the actual sign of Aquarius that need to be explored. In this chapter I discuss the myriad meanings behind the astrological sign of Aquarius. From these symbols, I provide a better picture of the New World we are now entering. Also, it will help you to understand the reason why we are experiencing such dramatic change in the Aquarian Age.

The Symbolic Meanings of Aquarius

To understand the times in which we are living, we must explore the symbolic meanings of the astrological sign of Aquarius. Astrology is an old method of understanding the Universe. It was developed by shamans and Priests of the ancient cultures. They developed it, in order to explain to other members of their society the important connection between the individual and the larger Universe. It has been used to predict the future of individuals and Society. There are several different versions of astrology. Each group that inherited it or created it had different environmental and cultural values. An example of this difference is shown in the Eastern and the Western forms of the Astrology system. For the sake of this section, I will be focusing on the Western form of Astrology.

What are the symbolic meanings of the sign of Aquarius? In terms of Western Astrology, Aquarius is a male sign ruled by the element of Air, the intellect, and the planet, Uranus. The symbol of Aquarius is often depicted as a man pouring water from vessel onto the Earth. Many people often associate this sign with water because there is water being poured. The water is actually only symbolic of the knowledge from the "gods of mankind" being spread to all people on the Earth. In other words, the pouring of spirit and knowledge onto the Earth, represents the spreading of universal truths that have been hidden. In astrology, Air is akin to the intellect. Therefore, we have in Aquarius the joining of the Mind and Spirit as higher thoughts and knowing from the universe becoming revealed. Aquarius is, also, related to a joining of the masculine with the feminine energies. As seen in the symbol of the male pouring the water which is symbolic of the feminine. This means both male and female energies will be restored to balance in the New Age. We have seen examples of this in the women's movement of the 1970s and the MeToo movement of the present day. Furthermore, the natural vibrations of Aquarius demand equality and balance in all areas of life so the Transition Period will be filled with events that demand this new paradigm of reality.

Uranus is closely associated with electricity and the Higher Mind. In mythological terms, Uranus was the first supreme god of Heaven, his partner was, Gaia, the goddess of the Earth. From them came the Titans and the Cyclops. The higher knowledge of Heaven, created by the original archetype of a supreme god invokes a greater understanding of Universal Truths. Uranus is the seventh planet in our solar system and the number seven is closely associated with Heaven. The information we are receiving is coming from Heaven. All the knowledge that has been sealed and locked away from Humanity for Millenia will be restored during the Age of Aquarius. One of these secrets is the chamber underneath the Sphinx in Egypt. The Age of Aquarius will bring humanity together in a global community as a whole. We will no longer have a need to separate ourselves from each other. The imbalances that were brought about in the previous Ages will be rectified and balanced once more. From what I've seen of the future age there will be Global Peace and healing for all. Unfortunately, we must pass through the last part of the transition. In order to know these things understanding the symbolic meanings associated with the astrological sign of Aquarius helps us to prepare for the New Age.

Please Stop the Insanity: Understanding the Transition Period.

The Transition Period we are going through right now brings many trials and tribulations for everyone on the planet. War, famine, disease, hatred, racism and classism are all elements of the things we must endure before we are completely in the Aquarian Age. This includes the inner struggles as well. This period of time is marked by those terrible dark things. Much of what I saw has already come to pass, but there are still a few more years left to go. All the people on this planet are in extreme jeopardy, because we have allowed those elitist groups of greed and lies to make us lose our focus on the Truth. Are we as a human race going to continue to allow these few individuals to dictate how we are going to live our lifes. During these dark times, we must all overcome our fears and release the shackles that have enslaved us for several Ages. We must learn to love and respect each other. I like to think of this time in history as an era of growing pains before entering into adulthood. In times of growth, we sometimes go through "growing pains" or lessons that aid us in becoming better and more responsible members of the planet Earth.

The Aquarian Age represents Humanity and shared community. It is, also, about freedom to be who you are without fear of persecution. The New Morality combines all of these aspects as we learn to respect and honor one another. Things like race, religion and sexual orientation will no longer be issues. Those things separated us from each other. We are meant to be coexisting as one species. Indeed, in time our skin tone will become more uniform as we relate and evolve.

We live in some exciting times! Hopefully, we will have the strength and courage to move up to the next level of Enlightenment and evolution. This age promises to be very utopian in its expression and openness. We just have to figure out how to get through the quagmire of insanity that we have created around ourselves. However, once we reach this new way of being, it will open doors to a newer and better kind of morality. It will empower people to be the best version of themselves.

Conclusion

Can we change the possibilities our futures? I believe we can change. Transition Periods between the ages are always difficult. If we all work together consciously to create a world of peace, equality, and freedom, there is a chance we can change our world. This book will aid in you in creating the new reality we all need to create.

I hope that the people that read my book will wake up and help prevent all governments and corporations from continuing from taking away our power. As a direct ambassador of the Council of the One and God. I can say that any government that denies basic equality and human rights is in direct violation of Heaven. I am the first of the Vanguard that has come to help the population to find the way to the New Age of Aquarius. Humanity has only begun to walk down the road of these evolutionary times. Let this book be a beacon for those that seek the truth and want to know a better way of being.

The things mentioned in this chapter are stepping stones to understanding the bigger picture of what is happening to us in these times. The Aquarian Age will bring about a great and lasting period of peace, equality, truth and freedom. Technology will continue to expand at an alarming rate and we will be able to travel both the wonders of the Stars and to the Great Within. Let's begin the journey together.

Getting Started

My first six months in the intergalactic classroom were spent learning and mastering grounding and centering. It was a very difficult time for me to adjust to my new regimen because I was living in two separate worlds. I had to learn how to counteract my lack of sleep with meditative techniques I learned in the classroom. I had my mundane life during the daytime and at night I had my spiritual world. Once I had adjusted to the new regimen the only difficult thing to work through was practicing what I have learned by myself. As I progressed into the other areas, they became easier for me to do the various techniques. In this chapter I will share with you my experiences for the first six months of my training. I will include what my teachers taught me and add my own perspective after working with these techniques for so many years.

Some of what is stated here was also stated to me by my teachers. They stated, "To begin it is important to establish a foundation of basic spiritual knowledge and practices. Whenever we build something to last it is necessary to have a solid base in order to allow for expansion." In this chapter I have laid the groundwork you will need with practices which can readily be built into a healthy spiritual life. Several angels and a couple disincarnate avatars taught me most of the information in this chapter. They are basic concepts of grounding and centering, psychic protection and astral projection.

The primary focus of this chapter is to provide a better understanding of the basics you will need to accomplish your spiritual goals. In the first two sections I share my training on the "how's" and "why's" of grounding and centering. The last two sections deal with meditations on psychic protection and astral projection. My teachers provided me with exercises on the varying subjects to help me practice these techniques and I have included them at the end of each section to help you. They will establish the beginnings of a useful foundation in spiritual practice.

Grounding and Centering

During my first week of the intergalactic classroom, my teachers taught me the importance of establishing a solid foundation in spiritual techniques. In order to create this, we must start with the basics. The most essential ingredient for getting started is to be grounded and centered. My personal experiences with these techniques were fun yet tedious at the same time because I had to unlearn certain aspects from what my grandmother and great-aunt had taught me. With practice and patience, I mastered these techniques and do most of them unconsciously today. Many people will have had great experiences already with these applications but any many others will find this information brand new. Practice is the key to all solid foundations in life. We must all be rooted deeply within ourselves and the planet in order to achieve the harmony that we crave. The process is relatively simple but it can take practice to master.

My teacher for the grounding and centering was Sananda or as he is also known, Jesus the Nazarene. He is an avatar and one of the manifestations of a cosmic consciousness of Christ. The information concerning avatars and cosmic consciousness will be discussed in detail in a later chapter. Sananda taught me everything that I share with you here. To ground and center yourself, begin with a simple breathing technique. Breathe in through your nose deeply filling your lungs and breathe out through your mouth. Do not hold your breath but let it flow continuously like a circle or an infinity symbol. It helps to visualize these things in the beginning until it becomes second nature. Breathing in this manner is important for three reasons. First it helps keep the balance of the energy within your body. Secondly it balances the energy between your heart and mind. Finally, it calms your mind so that you can hear that "little voice" or the voice of the higher self within you. The higher self is that part of your being that is connected to the source which is the highest expression of the life force that flows through everything. Breathing is the most important thing that we can do because we cannot survive without it. We can survive without food or water for several days but we cannot survive without breathing for more than a few moments. Practice this breathing in and out for several days whenever you find a moment of free time. In time your circular breathing will become like second nature to you.

The process of grounding is simply a matter of expanding your mind and visualizing a part of yourself going deep into the center of the Earth. To begin the grounding process you should be sitting, standing or lying down on your back. While you are breathing begin to visualize a part of yourself or a thread of light from yourself stretching deep into the Earth. As you breathe feel yourself going deeper into the Earth and let yourself become one with all of life. You will feel yourself expanding as you experience the interconnectedness to all things. The first time I experienced this it was quite overwhelming because I could literally feel everything around me. With more practice you can bond all the way down to the molecular level of all things on the planet Earth. Only go as far as you feel comfortable. Using your cord or piece of your metaphorical self, latch on to wherever you are in the earth. If you have done correctly you cannot be moved by anyone or anything outside of yourself.

Now return to yourself. Continue the circular breathing go within yourself and find your center. Your center is that place where only you can go. Nothing from the external world may enter here. If you can't find your Center it can be anything from simple to very complex. It is the safe place that belongs only to you inside of your heart. It is completely who you are in the quiet of your soul. My teacher, Sananda, worked for a long time on this area because I could not understand this concept. Finally, I created the place inside the deepest part of my heart chakra with a beautiful willow tree in a field of wildflowers next to a tiny brook. I use this place for centering but also for calming. Once you have created your center you can move onto the more advanced techniques. Below are the exercises I used to perfect my understanding and practice of grounding and centering.

Exercise

1. Practice your daily breathing. Remember to keep it continuous and flowing like an infinity symbol. The breathing will help you later with all meditations.
2. Practice the grounding exercise every morning when you get up.
3. Practice the centering exercise daily at least three times per day until it becomes second nature.

Advanced Grounding and Centering Techniques

My teacher, Sananda, began teaching us the advanced techniques after he was satisfied that we had mastered the basics. He said, "There are several ways in which you can do it. Some of these techniques will enable you to expand your consciousness. Hugging a tree, for instance, is just one simple method to ground and center. Walking or standing in the grass while doing mudras is very helpful." For those who do not know, mudras are symbolic gestures with hands, arms and legs that add special significance to the ritual you are performing. The Sufis, an Asian religious order, utilize them with great success in their dancing rituals. There is no right or wrong way with these techniques. As with most things in life, we all follow our own paths to Enlightenment and these are only a few of the techniques that were passed on to me. What I will share with you is a few of the simpler methods.

The simplest way by far is to meditate while walking through nature. This technique is easy to do and very calming at the same time. While you are walking, begin with the continuous breathing. Once you have acquired relaxation and quieted your mind, you will begin to feel the energy of Life flowing around you. You feel every muscle in your body as you were walking. To feel the energy flows around you simply expand your awareness beyond your physical body. As you expand your personal field outward, you begin to feel the life force of everything.

Another method of advanced grounding and centering is the earth bonding meditation. It is similar to the above method except or you are not walking. Begin by lying down in the grass or sitting underneath a tree. Breathe in a circular manner relax your body and visualize a cord of yourself going deep into the Earth. Now bring your consciousness back to yourself. Slowly begin to expand your awareness. Allow yourself to feel the world around you. You will feel the pulse of the life force that flows through everything. Go deeper still until you feel the molecular bonds. Now expand your awareness outwards. Slowly begin to feel every blade of grass and every leaf in the tree. Feel your body flowing in sync with the life around you. This technique is very powerful because it gives you a deep connection to Mother Earth.

The next method is all the earth mudra meditation. It is similar to the "mountain stance" a basic movement taught in yoga. It is simply a variation of the earth bonding meditation. Though this technique is more advanced than the original, it shares many of the same concepts in grounding and centering. To begin the process, stand in the grass with your legs about shoulder length apart. Raise your arms over your head with the palms of your hands inwards and up. Now bring your palms together over your head and bring them down over your heart. Next bend down and touch the earth with your palms. Say a small prayer to Mother Earth and ask her to help you by allowing some of her energy to flow up into your body. Bring that energy up into your heart center by standing erect with your palms together over your heart. Next, keeping your palms together bring your hand back over your head. Now say a prayer to the Father in Heaven and ask to share the energy of Air and Light with you. Now visualize the energy going with your hands together. Bring them down to your heart center. Feel and visualize the two energies as they combine to create a synergy within your heart. Say a prayer of gratitude to the father and the mother and thank them for the abundance of gifts that they have given you. If you are in a rush this meditation is excellent for grounding and centering simply because it only takes a few moments.

All of these techniques are relatively easy to do and are great for getting a quick energy burst. They also provide a good beginning for your foundation and daily spiritual practices. I recommend practicing them whenever you feel like it but especially after you feel comfortable with yourself and your body. The exercise below will be a good starting point for you to practice these Advanced Techniques of grounding and centering.

Exercise

1. Take a walk in nature preferably where there is little or no intrusions from the urban environment. Prepare yourself by doing the continuous breathing. Begin your walk in nature. During your walk you want to make sure that you feel them every muscle in your body that you are using to walk. Focusing on the feeling all the muscles getting oxygen so they can do their duties. Feel your body relaxing as you deepen your focus. Begin to expand your awareness from your personal body to the world around you. Remember to remain with the continuous breathing. When you are done bring your awareness back into your body and thank the Earth for its time.

2. For the Earth Bonding Meditation, begin by lying down in the grass or sitting under a tree. Begin with continuous breathing. Utilizing the continuous breath and visualization, focus your awareness at your feet. Feel them relax as you bring oxygen to the area. Now move up slowly until you have relaxed every muscle in your body. Once you have completely relaxed visualize a cord of energy from yourself going deep down into the Earth to anchor yourself. Now bring your awareness back to your body.

3. Begin the Earth mudra meditation. Stand in the grass with your legs shoulder length apart. While doing the continuous breathing Bring both arms over your head with your palms turned inwards and upwards. Once they are above your head bring your hands together Palm to Palm. From this position say a little prayer to the Father and ask him to share some energy with you. Now you will bring your hands over your heart to anchor that energy that you have received in your heart. Now been down and put your palms of your hand down on the earth. Say a prayer to Mother Earth asking her to share some energy with you. Now bring yourself to a standing position and clasp your hands Palm to Palm over your heart now say a prayer of Thanksgiving to Father and the Mother. Ask that the energies be joined together so you may become balanced.

Psychic Protection

In The intergalactic classroom, the Archangel Michael was the teacher for this section. He said, "There are many things in your world that can be dangerous or even threatening. Many of you have encountered what has been toxic or draining in the form of a person or thing. i.e. psychic vampires and toxic people. They can wreak havoc on your energy field and may even cause you bodily harm. There is also the harm that comes indirectly from the world around you. How can you protect yourself from these things? As was mentioned earlier by my brother Cherubim, there is an electromagnetic field that surrounds you. All human beings have a energy field around their bodies. They all have bioelectric energy sending signals to different parts of the body from the brain. This field is generated by your nervous system. For most people this energy field extends out from their body about 3 to 6 feet. It is this field that gets so adversely affected by the negative environments or people that are around you."

He continued, "For sensitives, those people with an active intuition, being in a toxic psychic environment can be almost deadly because they can pick up more things about a place or person than someone with the less conscious gift." It is important to learn how to protect yourself from these influences or it could lead to a variety of problems like depression, paranoia, and insomnia. For example, you could encounter a toxic person or psychic vampire, and if you do not know how to shield yourself from them, you might feel devastated. The toxic person could drain you to the point of listlessness and the psychic vampire could very well take everything you have to offer. Another example might come in the form of a place with tremendous negative energy. If you do not have proper Protections in place it could leave you off balance and befuddled.

Psychic protection is basically about boundaries and what you will allow to happen to your energetic fields. This section is about learning some techniques that can assist you in protecting yourself and your boundaries. Always remember to use the foundation of grounding and centering in all that you do.

Visualization plays a major role in developing adequate defenses. The mind is the greatest tool we have and through it we can generate just about anything. The easiest form of psychic defense is visualizing a bubble of white light surrounding your body. Next using the grounding techniques learned earlier in this chapter, you can borrow some energy from the Earth to strengthen it and yourself. After a few seconds or moments, you should be able to feel the bubble around you. If you need to protect yourself further, I recommend layering your bubble with extra energy from the Earth. By doing the earth mudra meditation you can move those added energies into the psychic shield around you.

Another example of protecting yourself from psychic harm is similar to magnetizing yourself. To magnetize yourself visualize little white flames around every part of your body. Next, you should visualize what you would like drawn to you like a person place or thing. See white flames around the object as you are holding it in your hands. I recommend starting out with something simple and inanimate for practice like a pen or a pebble. It will take one to two days but the object will come to you. When you harden your auric field, it is similar to magnetizing, with one difference, you do not visualize an object to attract. To harden your auric field, imagine little flames of white light all around your body. You may have to concentrate on this for a bit because it can be difficult at first but with practice it will become like second nature to you. Once you have hardened your aura it will be able to protect you from most psychic harm but it will not make you invulnerable. I recommend this technique if you know you will be going into a very negative environment.

The most important thing to remember is to laugh. When you are in a highly charged negative situation the best thing you can do is laugh. Laughter, like crying, is extraordinarily cathartic, and it can dramatically shift any energy. Most people will be disarmed by laughter during a stressful situation. Many of the Masters that taught me recommended that you take on an air of childlike innocence so negativity just flows off your psychic shield. Laughing may seem silly but trust me it works. Simply laughing at a very tense moment can diffuse the negativity held there. It works to help restore the equilibrium in any situation. Developing a positive attitude with plenty of laughter can go a long way in your personal psychic protection.

Developing a strong psychic defense is tantamount to protecting yourself from those that would cause you harm. As you gain in strength and understanding about yourself and your gifts these techniques will become increasingly important. The exercises below provide a good base from which you can begin the process of laying part of your spiritual foundation. Not only will these protect you but they will protect those around you as well.

Exercise

1. To begin practice building the white bubble starting with the continuous breath. Now visualize a white bubble surrounding your body. Practice making your Shield Stronger by integrating the earth mudra meditation to pull an extra energy from the earth and the air.
2. To harden your auric field by using the continuous breathing technique. Visualize little flames of white light joining together over every inch of your body. Once you have accomplished this task or a field will be in 24 to 36 hours.
3. Laugh. Whenever you feel the need to laugh do it. Remember there does not have to be a reason to laugh.since it is related to emotions and not the mind.

Astral Projection

Astral projection was one of the first things I learned during my time in the intergalactic classroom. The Archangel Michael taught it.to me on that eventful night when he took me on a tour of the universe. Astral projection Is simply the ability to allow your spirit to leave the body. When your spirit is released from its physical bonds you can explore many wonderful places within the multiple dimensions of the universe. If you have ever awakened from a dream feeling weary then you might have unconsciously astraly projected. It is important for the spirit to wander and all of us do this at some point or another.

The Archangel Michael showed me the easiest way to astral project. The following is the information that I received from him telepathically. He placed his hands upon my temples and I felt a rush of information being poured into my mind. This is what I received: while lying down place yourself in a meditative state with the continuous breathing. Allow your essence or Spirit self to float upwards. You will feel a tingling sensation as you float outside your physical form. Once you're out of your body make sure that you have a silver cord attached to your power area. The silver cord is a constant connection to your physical form and it will help to guide you back at the end of your travels. Now you are ready to explore the universe. All of this will take some practice.

There are a couple of obstacles to overcome in the first few sessions. First the feeling of disorientation while floating above your body may be a bit frightening because it is a new sensation that we are not used to experiencing. Another obstacle is to realize that the laws of the physical world no longer apply in the higher planes. For instance, you are now able to pass through objects like a ghost and you can travel anywhere you want to go at the speed of a thought. Just think about where you want to be and you will be there in the same instant. Once you have overcome these obstacles it will be much easier for you to explore the universe.

Astral projection is fun because it can provide you with a sense of flying. In fact, a flying dream usually indicates your subconscious interpretation of an astral Journey. Now, I am so proficient in astral journeys, I can just be sitting in a meditative state and leave my body. It has become like second nature to me. It combines most of the other techniques mentioned in this chapter. For instance, the continuous breathing, grounding and psychic protection all play important roles in astral projection. Below I have provided an exercise to begin your own astral journey.

Exercise

1. Practice projecting your spirit out of your body. Began by using the continuous breathing to bring yourself into a meditative state. Feel yourself floating up and out-of-your body. Remember this feeling can be very disconcerting at first because it is entirely new. Experiment with astral traveling by thinking about where you want to go. Remember when you are ready to return just follow the silver cord back to your physical body.

Conclusion

The things mentioned in this chapter are primarily to guide you in establishing a solid practicum for your spiritual evolution. They are all important and interconnected. For example, you need to be grounded and centered in order to work with the other techniques. With practice and discipline these tools will become an essential element to the foundation you are creating. The Aquarian Age will offer more expanded opportunities to access these gifts and talents. The closer we get to the end of the transition the more challenges we will face. We will have to be more steadfast in our knowledge and understanding of what we have learned. It will also open new doorways in eliminating the concepts of hatred and intolerance created during the last century of the Picsean Age.

The Psychic Abilities and Their Seven Levels

Psychic abilities and their seven levels were taught to us in the second half of the first year. Our teacher for this area was the Archangel Gabriel. The information she provided us gave us yet another Stone in the foundation of spiritual practices for the Aquarian Age. I was luckier than some of the others because I had already learned some of this from my grandmother. I remember practicing on others in my daily life to see how much the information was accurate. I have always been a "Doubting Thomas" unless I see it with my eyes. I doubt it is true. All of the information in this chapter is relevant to what is coming in the Aquarian Age, because it will be needed to bridge the gaps and barriers that have existed since the Piscean Age.

We all have psychic abilities to some degree maybe you've had a feeling of déjà vu or felt like it would be a bad idea to do something. All of these strange occurrences and many more are psychic in nature. The Psychic abilities are closely tied to the intuitive side of the brain. Many people have probably heard of Clairvoyance or Clairaudience but all the abilities are becoming more prevalent in the New Age. Most people have at least one of these gifts to varying degrees and a few of us have all of of them. As we move into the Aquarian Age the veil between the dimensions is growing thinner. In the New Age there is no separation between the dimension of 3rd through 5th. We have seen or will see our abilities to see, hear, taste, smell and know increasing as we move more into the higher frequencies.

The seven levels of psychic development illustrates the evolution of these gifts. Everyone falls somewhere within the 7 levels and you can progress into higher levels with practice and discipline. In this chapter, I also explain what my teacher taught me with each of the seven levels of psychic abilities. Once the knowledge is integrated into the seven levels, it is easier to understand the larger universe. These things are just another Stone in the foundation you are learning for your spiritual growth. It is my hope this chapter will help you in your journey towards your Higher Self in the New Age.

The Eight Aspects of Psychic Ability

The Eight Aspects of Psychic Ability are the first part of the training I received from Archangel Gabriel. Those abilities are Clairvoyance, Clairaudience, Clairsentience, Clairempathy, Clairtangency, Clairsaliency, Clairgustance and Claircognizance. The Archangel Gabriel stated "One of the greatest things about the Psychic Aspects is the ability to experience things from a higher vibration." These Aspects grant those awakening to see, hear, know, smell, and taste information from the Higher Dimensions. All of them are dramatically increasing as we move further into the Aquarian Age.

Clairvoyance is the ability to see clearly into other Realms or to see things as they really are. It can be paired with precognition to help see glimpses of possible futures. The Universe is made up of multiple dimensions, and we have aspects of all of them within ourselves. For example, the fourth dimension is where most people that are no longer in body go after their physical form dies. The higher dimensions have the Angelic Realms and many of the Extraterrestrial Races. Basically, anything you might see with your Third Eye is clairvoyance. Most people have already experienced clairvoyance to some degree over the years. We will all begin to notice an increase in our Clairvoyance as the years progress.

Another form of the Psychic Ability is Clairaudience and this is basically to clearly hear things. When we receive messages coming from a Higher Dimension, this is Clairaudience. Many beings from a Higher Plane are trying to communicate with us. When we decide to listen we might be able to live in a better and safer world. Some examples of clairaudience are hearing your name being called but nobody is around you or you are about to do something you should not and you hear a strong "Stop!". In the New Age there is actually a New Chakra being activated and anchored in the back of the head specifically bringing in Clairaudience. We should all be able to communicate with Higher Dimensional beings. It also acts as a kind of universal translator. As we enter into the Aquarian Age it will be important to understand and acknowledge all the messages we are receiving from Heaven.

The next thing is claircognizance and it is the ability clearly know things. This ability will manifest itself as just knowing something without ever really studying anything about the subject matter. Basically, you are tapping into the Akashic Records from a higher plane of knowing. With any ability it can be honed with practice. I have this for instance and ideas and knowledge just come to me. It is how I write and I think a lot of people have this as an intuitive knowing. As we enter into the Aquarian Age it will become prevalent for people to know the right thing or wrong thing to do at a certain time.

Clairempathy is the ability to know how a person is feeling. This is one of the unique gifts. Everyone has this ability but few actually use it in this day and age. You have to be very careful because you can just pick up emotions very strongly. It can affect you on a very deep level if you do not shield yourself. It deals with the emotional plane so basically it means you can tap into the emotional field of other people. The Emotional Aura Field is the second energy layer around the physical body. You are able to pick up on emotions very easily. Just be sure when you are doing it you are shielded and protected. It is a wonderful gift if you are in the healing field.

The next Ability is Clairsentience It is similar to Clairempathy in the sense that you feel what the person is feeling. However, it is much more physical in nature. Some other things you might experience is a gut feeling. So, it's really affecting you through the etheric energy field. I have experienced it especially when I'm working on another body. I get a sense when I am doing body work or energy work. I can sense where the blocks are in the other person's body.

The next ability is Clairtangency. It is clear touching. All that really means is when you touch an object of someone you can pick up on their energy fields. It is also known as psychometry. When you touch something from another's energy field, you can see or feel what is going on with them. Many "psychics" use this ability when they read another person. It can definitely help in solving mysteries surrounding somebody.

Clairsalience is the next Psychic Ability. It is simply clear smelling. For instance, you might smell something in the air that reminds you of somebody that has crossed over to other planes. Many of the beings from the Higher Dimensions also have very distinctive smells. Entering into the New Age will probably find more people getting a keener sense of smell.

The last Psychic Ability coming through strongly in the New Age is Clairgustance. It is clear tasting. You are able to taste something like it was right in your mouth. For instance, somebody from your past that made a dish you loved you will experience the tasted memory of that person in your mouth. It is a happy memory that triggers a cellular memory. It means the person from that higher dimension is around you.

Anything can be abuse if you have a negative intention. Therefore, always strive to think happy thoughts and intentions when using your abilities. All of these abilities should be used to help others along the Path. It is so important to create new understanding of love and compassion with everyone. We all have one or more of these gifts to some extent and they will continue to grow and develop at an alarming rate. We must all learn to coexist with each other. I have provided some exercises for everyone to work on developing their Psychic Abilities

Exercise

1. Determine what gifts you have. Do the circular breathing and open your heart and your mind to feel and listen to the Higher Dimensions. The answers will come to you.
2. Develop your nascent gifts by keeping a journal of your experiences so you can identify what they are.
3. Still your mind during your grounding and centering exercises so you can learn what you need to learn from your ancestors and guides.

The Seven Levels of Psychic Development

Moving from the first section about psychic abilities, we head into the second area of the seven levels of the Psychic Development. There are seven specific areas which will help to determine your natural abilities. Once we know where our gifts lie within the different stages, it is easier to master those gifts. The seven levels are psychic development are:

1. Psychic,
2. Seer,
3. Channel,
4. Medium,
5. Visionary,
6. Creator, and
7. Avatar.

All of the levels contain 7 more stages of understanding and ability. The seven stages are:

1. Beginner,
2. Novice,
3. Apprentice,
4. Journeyman,
5. Advanced Journeyman,
6. Master, and
7. Adept Master.

For instance, I am a Stage 7 Medium. This means I can access the Higher Dimensions and interact with entities without going into a trance. With study and discipline, we can all learn to move up the levels to our highest development. These talents will become increasingly important as the veil between the dimensions get thinner and the world becomes smaller. In biology, our physical bodies actually have areas that manage the psychic abilities. The pituitary, pineal and Hypothalamus glands are those glands that promote psychic ability in humans. Just like any other part or system in the body these glands will become more prominent as we move further into the Aquarian Age. A manifestation of the Aquarian Age will be a better understanding of each other and the world around us.

The first level is Psychic. People with these gifts have a heightened intuitive capacity or "sixth sense". A person with psychic abilities will usually know who is calling them before they answer the phone or get the sense to call a friend in need. This stage is very frustrating at the best of times and completely unreliable at the worst of times especially in the earlier stages of development. People on this level will get flashes of insight but they are rare and seemingly random. With training, one can figure out what area of the brain is functioning and develop it. Given time and patience you can train yourself access to higher and higher levels of knowing to newer more elevated levels of Consciousness. The aspects of psychic ability that are discussed earlier work fluidly in this level. For example, the third stage psychic might have a very active Clairvoyant ability. For example, it allows them to find things psychically when they are lost.

The second level is Seer. A Seer is someone who gets Visions about people or events in the past, present or future. Seers of all the categories usually go into a trance and have a clairvoyant experience of whatever or whomever they are looking into at the time. Initially, a Seer will have to use tools like mirrors or crystal balls to see. The seeing is completely uncontrollable at the early stages. It is also called the "Sight" by some of the older religions. Through training and experience the Seer can access and control the path they wish to see. For example, a Fifth Stage Seer will probably need a personal object and use a combination of Clairvoyance and Clairtangency to see a clear picture of what the need to see. They have more conscious control about what is happening when the seer answers to questions.

Most people have heard of channeling. Basically, channeling is the ability to allow an entity from a higher dimensional plane to speak or work through you. These spirits beyond yourself usually have some message or gift to give to others. This level of psychic ability works the same way as the previous levels. It has seven stages of awareness "Stage 1" being the lowest to "Stage 7" being the Adept ability. In the lower stages you do not have conscious control over what is coming through. I have encountered many alleged Channeler's that claimed they were channeling a higher Dimensional being when in fact they were only expressing themselves from their Ego. It is vitally important for any channel to be completely clear of their ego when they are in channel to prevent any negativity or past personal stuff to come up. At the higher stages of channeling the person will actually take on personality characteristics like hand and facial gestures. They will also speak in a different voice. You should train and study to develop the protection to yourself and others.

The next level of psychic development is medium. Medium is similar to channeling, since you are contacting entities of a higher Dimension. The difference is the medium does not need to allow the entity into their body. Some of the people in this country have heard of mediums. For example, John Edwards is a Stage 6 Medium. Most mediums tend to stick with deceased relatives but they can communicate with beings from the Higher Dimensions as well. Again, at the lower stages one must go into a trance in order to communicate with the entities but as one trains and masters theirs gifts, they can achieve communion without trances. At the higher levels the spirits will converse with you in real time. It is like you exist in two worlds at once. With this gift you are able to interact with the Higher Dimensions, allowing you to access information you will need for the New Age.

The next level is the Visionary. Visionaries have a highly developed clairvoyant ability which allows them to see all the possible outcomes. Their Third Eye is very open. At the lower levels this ability will come as dreams and flashes of a personal nature such as déjà vu. The experiences in Dreamtime are more vivid and real for someone with a Visionary gift. At the higher levels the Visions are accompanied by trances and usually involve a larger Community or population.

The next level is the Creator. They can create things seemingly out of nowhere, mainly from the astral plane. Their Creations can be anything from manifesting some fish to eat to whatever they want or need at the time. At the lower levels the Creator has the basic creative skills down. Anything related to the arts and science or where creating something new is required. Two good examples of Creators are Albert Einstein and William Shakespeare. Creators are of great importance as we move into the Aquarian Age because they are able to define the new ways of being that are coming into consciousness. As with all the other levels practice until you attain a higher level of functioning.

The last level is the Avatar. The Avatar has the ability to access all the other levels with ease and can function in any capacity. In other words, they are able to have visions of the future, create new technology, and interact with the Higher Dimensions without any difficulty. Jesus of Nazareth or Siddhartha are good examples of people that were functioning on the Avatar level of psychic ability. They were very powerful psychics, healers, teachers and leaders in our world. Very few people have been born to the seventh level due to the higher amount of responsibility. Since entering into the Aquarian Age, we are all beginning to access this Avatar ability. We are all Awakening and beginning to access the the Christ Consciousness.

These gifts are very special and we all have most of them to some extent. As we enter the Aquarian Age, it will become more important to know where your talents lie in regards to Psychic Ability. We can no longer deny ourselves because they are in all of us. We must all find where we lay within the various levels so we can all participate in the Galactic Federation. We are moving forward into the New Age and these gifts will become more conscious to us. Our connection to each other in the higher planes of existence will deepen our connectedness to each other. By increasing our awareness and training ourselves in the various levels, we can begin to restore balance to the entire planet. We are all united through our individual sparks of Divinity. These sparks manifest as our psychic abilities and spiritual understanding.

In conclusion the psychic abilities and seven levels of the psychic development are important abilities that we are creating. All of the levels and abilities work together closely in unison or separately as the need arises. It will become increasingly important to be honest with yourself and others. These abilities promote frankness in individuals because we are opening ourselves to the larger Universe. It is all part of becoming the global community and building a world based upon acceptance and understanding. Use what you have learned here with wisdom and respect for all life.

The Seven Levels of
Soul Development

My teachers for this lesson were Quan Yin and Osiris. They said "Everything in this universe recycles itself. It continues to flow back around into the circle of life. Death is nothing more than a beginning." I mentioned in the last chapter most disincarnate beings exist in the fourth dimension. When you die you usually go here to wait until it is time for your return to the physical plane. While there, you learn from your experiences and continue the process of evolving towards the Source. Some Souls even assist those still in this dimension through guidance as guardian angels or spirit guides. Each time you return to the physical plane you have lessons to be learned that brings you closer to God or the Source.

It is arrogant to presume that you are outside the influences of the world around you. What makes you so special that you are above and beyond the confines of the basic laws of Universe? How would you feel if you have to sit around and wait for a "Judgement Day"? It sounds rather boring to me. How can you assume to know what takes place once your physical form dies? Your soul is the vibrant part of yourself that is connected to a life in the Universe and it is never-ending. The concept of reincarnation has been around in most religions for millenia. In 333 A.D. there was a council held in Assisi, Italy. It was during this time the final formula for the Catholic Church was decided on by men in power. They discarded large portions of the writings and certain beliefs that did not fit in with their view of the world. Reincarnation was deemed inappropriate for the fledgling Church at the time. Even though most of the other sects of Christianity accepted this concept from the writings of the original Gospel. The religious caste and the Roman Emperor did not want to believe they might come back as peasants. By removing this important aspect of thought from the text of the Bible, it created a tremendous void in all people. It separated them from all other life. It also removed the responsibility to maintain balance and be good stewards of the planet.

During the Aquarian Age, all of the truths are being rediscovered. Reincarnation is one of these truths. Each soul is an individual expression of the Divine. There are seven levels of every soul with 49 plus 1 lifetimes within each level. These levels are divided into categories based upon the level of learning a soul is here to learn.

In this chapter I discuss the seven levels of Soul Development. I have named them as I was taught in The Intergalactic Classroom and have included my own interpretation to help others understand the concept. They are:

1. Nomadic / Baby,
2. Tribal/Child,
3. Village/Grade School,
4. Town/Teenager,
5. individual/College,
6. Community Service/Masters, and
7. Global Service/Doctorate.

Each lifetime contains many lessons. The more we avoid these lessons the more they will continue to pop-up until we have learned the lesson.

Throughout this chapter, I make reference to astrological signs. Astrology is the study of the stars to aid in predicting an individual's lessons in life. It has a chart that is divided into twelve sections which corresponds to the twelve different signs. Each sign is associated with identifying personality traits. Both Eastern and Western philosophies have twelve signs to represent the various members of society. They all relate to reincarnation because it is believed individuals reincarnate around the wheel of astrology to learn the different lessons from each sign.

The first level of Soul Development is called the Nomad, but I prefer to call it the Baby level. At this stage the soul is very young. The primary purpose of this level is to learn to experience life in a physical form. Everything is new and wonderful. The soul experiences all things for the first time. These souls are freshly separated from the Source. This newness to life leaves them confused but eager to experience all there is in life. In terms of astrology, the individual is more likely to be born in the signs of Aries, Taurus or Gemini which represent the beginnings of Life in astrology. Most younger souls choose to experience a variety of things to enjoy the physical world. This level of development is closely tied to the *Soul Family*. The *Soul Family* is that group which we continually reincarnate with in order to learn the greatest lessons. They identify with this Family unit and can be easily manipulated by it. Younger souls are easily swayed by others and will not have a strong sense of individuality. Most of the young Souls stopped being born after 1970.

The second level of Soul Development is known as the Tribal Level. I refer to it as the Child Stage of the Soul. The primary purpose of this level of development is to understand life through basic interaction with others. At this level the soul closely identifies with smaller groups beyond the *soul family*. They become part of a group consciousness. These are often referred to as *Soul Groups*. They usually consist of groups of friends that have reincarnated together as a gang or tribe in order to learn and assist each other in life lessons. Many *Soul Groups* formed during to these lifetime's will follow the soul throughout its journey back to the Source. Most people is this second level are prone to getting tattoos and body piercing. Peer pressure is very prevalent in this level of development. In astrological terms this level is associated with Cancer, Leo, and Virgo.

Moving forward into the village or grade school level of the Soul we find development going towards greater consciousness in outer influences. The primary purpose of this level is to learn how to interact with the larger society. This is the level where we learn about the acceptable behavior of the larger culture. Most people of this level will follow the status quo. They believe fervently in the ideology of "it is their way or the highway" mentality. They go out of their way not to rock the boat and do whatever it takes to "fit" in with the larger society. The soul begins to learn lessons to help it understand more about the larger community. Here they move beyond the family and group levels into working with others in the society. There is a sense of right versus wrong, good versus evil or white versus black. They will be unwilling to compromise their belief systems based upon learned behaviors. In astrological terms this level is associated with the signs of Libra, Scorpio or Sagittarius.

The fourth level of Soul Development is called the City or as I like to call it the Teenage level. The primary focus for this level is to learn who you are as an individual and how you can express yourself to the larger world. People will begin to explore more about her spiritual nature's. Moving away from the status quo and towards a more profound understanding of their divine sparks. At this level people will explore a wide range of subjects such as creativity and spirituality. Some of the examples of exploration might be vegetarianism, gurus, alternative ways of healing. They still view things as black and white. As they progress upwards they will develop more towards freedom and individuality. Rebellion against the status quo is very pronounced at this level. Many activists and other Creative Expressionists are found at this level. I associate this level with high school because it is a time in our lives when we begin to bend and break the rules of society. They are finding their true soul identity. In terms of Astrology this level is associated with Capricorn, Aquarius and Pisces.

As we move into the fifth level of Soul Development, the expression of individuals is more pronounced. This level of soul development is referred to as the Individual/College level. Indeed, at this level, your soul is obtaining a college degree. Its primary purpose is to learn how to integrate your individualism back into service for the society at large. It is at this level that the soul begins to recognize and acknowledge Divine Sparks in others. They do not need to fit into society but have a strong desire to fix the problems that do exist. Expressing yourself in the fullness of your individual spark is very important. A person at this level already knows who they are in divine terms and they become keenly aware of the problems with their world. They also possess passionate energies to correct the problems they see. The need for right and wrong diminishes and the understanding of gray is confirmed. Furthermore there is a deeper understanding of one's individual spark. Astrologically speaking this level is associated any of the signs on the wheel.

The sixth level of Soul Development is about community service. At this level of development you are working on acquiring a Master's degree in the Soul through Selfless service to others. The soul has a vast pool of knowledge to draw from previous lifetimes. The primary purpose is about helping others to become empowered. The soul is driven to provide guidance and service to the larger community. A person at this level has great spiritual awareness and has little or no need for outside input. They are here to help others along their journey of soul development. Expression of the Divine is innate in these individuals. They understand that it is through empowering others that they receive the greatest satisfaction in life. The knowledge and experience from their past lives provide a strong base for making the best decision regarding the empowerment of others. In terms of astrology, these souls can be anywhere on the wheel of life but they will have a strong Aquarian or Pisces influence.

The seventh level of Soul Development is about global service. I relate it to getting your doctorate. The soul moves itself beyond the community and more towards global service. This group will strive to make changes in the world through service. The changes come about in a variety of methods but all of them raise awareness of some particular problem that exists. Some examples of people with this level of soul are Gandhi, the Dalai Lama, Martin Luther King Jr and, Mother Teresa. The Self has become less important and rectifying the problems of the world become more important. They bring awareness to all aspects of the world. There is also a better grasp of the Higher Mysteries at this level. These individuals carry a great deal of spiritual energy because their spark of divinity has joined with the larger connectedness of the source. Their flames are used to lead the world out of Darkness into the Light. These Souls fall under any sign which will best suit their mission.

All levels of the Soul are important because they are all aspects of the divine. Each is learning something that will bring the soul closer to the infinite. As we ascend the spiral staircases to higher understanding, we all learn the greatness of interconnection with each other and all life in the Universe. Our souls are progressing into something greater than we can comprehend. Moving into the Aquarian Age has created a great influx of older souls being born. This is happening for two reasons. First the human race as a species is evolving, Secondly the planet Earth is evolving too. Evolution towards a higher understanding is becoming more important in this New Age. These older souls are here to assist in the birthing process of the species and the planet. The Aquarian Age is about being able to express our authentic selves in freedom and equality. The patriarchal society of the Piscean Age is no longer feasible as we move into the New Age. Freedom to be who you are as long as you do not harm others. During this last part of the transition, there will be several of the higher levels of the Soul coming forward to lead the world out of the last vestiges of the Piscean Age. Below are some exercises to help you determine your level of soul.

Exercise

1. What are your beliefs? Write a credo. There is no wrong answer.
2. What level of soul are you? Determine this by reading what you have written.

The Importance of Understanding Your Past Lives

The higher you go in the development of your soul there are more lifetimes in which you can pool helpful information. All of your past, present and future lifetimes can be joined together into what is known as the *Constant Now*. The Constant Now is the loop of space and time that allows you to access the information you have learned from each lifetime so it can be utilized in the present moment. This section further explains past lives and how they all relate back to this life. Later I describe a new technique which I have developed to help you explore your past lives. I also discuss a meditative technique that was shared with me by my teachers. The Akashic Records are the records of all your lifetimes.

A common problem that many people have with past lives is gender. The soul is sexless or androgynous. It comes from the Source and is both sexes. Therefore, many people will incarnate as both male and female during their multiple incarnations. It all depends upon what lessons you need to learn at that time. From these lessons, you choose how you want to learn by selecting what things you will need in your life. For instance, your lesson may be learning how to share your wealth with others so you will incarnate into a life of stinginess with your material wealth. All of the lessons an individual learns at the various levels of development relate back to their understanding of life.

Another area of confusion for some people is race. By "race," I am referring to the common error of most people classifying people into skin tones. A soul does not have a skin coloration since it is vibrating at a higher frequency. In the higher Dimensions we are all equal. There is no class, race, religion, gender, or sexual orientation. The soul just is. All the things we place such great value on in the mundane world mean nothing in the Higher Dimensions.

In other words, it is highly probable that you have rarely been anyone of consequence. In fact, you are more likely to have been a female peasant or a slave of a different race. For example, I was an African female slave in Louisiana two lifetimes ago. All souls reincarnate with an equal balance between male and female. Some of these lifetimes carry over to the present lifetime because you did not complete all of the lessons you needed to learn. There are several techniques used to help you learn about your past lifetimes.

The first technique to aid you in accessing your past lives was developed by me during my many years as a healer. It allows you to enter into the cellular memories of your past lives through energetic means. It works on the premise that the body is balanced energy surrounding your soul manifesting itself in a physical shell. Therefore, the cells of the body hold the memories of all past lives your soul has lived. The physical body is connected to the Etheric body and we can access it through this technique. Generally, they are only glimpses of past traumas or good feelings. It is unlikely you would be able to know everything about a specific life using this technique. I worked with many clients to help them resolve the trauma held in their bodies from past lives.

It was designed to help people work through their emotional and spiritual wounds. I integrated some of the techniques in the Intergalactic Classroom with my own personal style of energetic facilitation. It proved to be very successful in helping my clients to live more open and free lives. The only time I encountered problems occurred when a client was taking a pharmaceutical to help them cope with their emotions. In order for anyone to fully express all the things you have experienced as a soul it is important to be able to access the full gamut of your emotions and experiences. This technique is ideally suited to healing spiritual and emotional traumas. There are many techniques in modern times that are used to help people explore their past lives. Some of these are merely guided meditation and they can provide a useful way to explore what you need to know.

In conclusion reincarnation is an integral part to the cycle of all souls as we ascend the metaphorical staircase to the Source. In fact, it is accepted in most of the world religions. In the Intergalactic Classroom I was taught the Seven Levels of Soul Development. Each of these levels has approximately fifty lifetimes all together. We must all live through the different lessons of each lifetime. The more experience we accumulate over our various lessons from the past the better to help others on their path.

Extraterrestrials and the Spiritual Hierarchy

The universe is made up of a multitude of microcosms and macrocosms. Within each of those realities exists an infinite number of life-forms. Billions of years ago there were thousands of sentient life-forms that spanned the Milky Way galaxy. Most of them began near the Galactic Core. There was only the void and then the Source had a thought and spoke. Light was created. So much light in fact it began to expand. The Source of All Life expanded to create new species. Some species became extinct as they failed in experimentation. The ones that survived advanced and became the caretakers of this Galaxy. Those aliens that remained serve the younger races in their evolution.

The nine major extraterrestrial races that remained behind came to be known as the Lords of Order and the Lords of Chaos. They are not really at odds with each other but try to maintain the Natural Balance of the Universe. They are considered to be the Watchers and Guardians of the younger species.

This chapter reveals and explains the spiritual hierarchy and all the entities who are involved. I actually spent a year-and-a-half on this information. I have condensed it down to the nine major races that are involved in the spiritual hierarchy so I cannot go into as much detail as I would like. The Archangel Gabriel and several different extraterrestrial races were my teachers of this class. We learned about the many other alien races that have been interacting with Humanity throughout most of our history.

Earlier I stated I will cover all the major older races in our Galaxy. These ET's have been around our planet for hundreds of millions of years. These races are divided into two categories (1) the Ancients and (2) The Elder Races. The only significant difference between them is how long they have been traveling the Galaxy.

The nine major races of extraterrestrials are the Sirians, the Pleiadians, the Lyrans, the Annu'naki, the Acturans, the Orallens, the Col'Notaros, the Zeta Reticulans, and the Lizarians. The Orions are actually the Orallens and the Col'Notaros. They were divided during the last great war of heaven over 50 million years ago. The ancient races are the Sirians, the Pleiadians, the Lyrans and the Annu'naki. The Elder races are the Arcturians, the Orallens, the Col'Notaros, the Zetas Reticulans and the Lizarians. These races are further subdivided by the pathways in which they return to Source. Those are Order and Chaos or Light and Dark. These different spiritual paths mark the way to how these races serve on the various councils.

This chapter is divided into the nine extraterrestrial races and the thirteen councils of spiritual hierarchy. They are important because they deal with all aspects of spiritual life. There are two important factors regarding extra extraterrestrials to keep in mind.

1. their continued involvement with humanity in this planet, and
2. knowing where they fall on the respective councils.

To help clarify the primary functions and attributes of each alien race I have added bullets to shorten the exposition. I have also done this for the functions of each council group. There are also several diagrams scattered throughout to provide visual effect on the basis of the council's designation. All of this will help us to grasp the nine major extraterrestrial races and the different council in the Hierarchy.

The Extraterrestrial Races

There are multiple numbers of extraterrestrial races in this universe. In this section Chapter 4 I discuss the oldest races among them. They have been around since time began and they have been travelling the stars for eons. These races are very familiar to the minds of humanity because they have been interacting with us in direct or indirect ways for most of our history. My teacher the Archangel Gabriel was very specific about these nine older alien races. The oldest races are often referred to as the "Ancient Ones." There are three things that separate the ancient races from the elder races. First, they have been space faring for several billions of years. Second, they have evolved to the point of simply being energy forms though they can appear in the 3rd dimension when the need arises. Third there are very few of them left because they no longer have a need to breed. Below, I provided a diagram that separates the two categories.

Diagram 1a

The Ancient Ones

Sirians	Pleiadian	Lyrans	Annu" Naki

The Elders

Arcturans	Orallens	Col'Notaros	Zeta Reticulans	Lizarians

The other five races are often referred to as the "Elder Races." They are the Arcturans, the Orallens, the Col'Notaros, the Zeta Reticulans, and the Lizarians. They are referred to as the Elders because they have been traveling in space for millions of years. They are very Advanced on the scales of spirituality, evolution and technology. While they have not been gone completely over to the energetic side, their frequencies vibrate well beyond the fifth dimension. Due to their advanced level of evolution they can also no longer produce offspring. They are so spiritually advanced that their connection to the source is constant.

The Ancient Ones

Diagram 1B

Sirians	Pleiadians	Lyrans	Annu'Naki

The first and oldest of the major ancient extraterrestrial races is the Sirians. They originated in the Sirian Star System about 3 ½ billion years ago. The star systems consist of Sirius A and B. They began to explore space about 2.4 billion years ago. They are the progenitors of several of the younger species. Since the Sirians have evolved beyond the point of physical manifestation, they rarely appear to the younger species. There are very few of their species left since most of them have returned to the Source. As far as I know only a few hundred of them still linger to serve the younger races and the Spiritual Hierarchy. Their homeworld is Sn'Anto'Forn the major system in the Sirius A Cluster. The homeworld for Sirius B is known as Sn'Bota'Forn. If you do encounter them on your journey they might appear as balls of flaming white fire or as tall bald men. They hang out in the 7th and 8th dimensions. They no longer have the need for starships since they can travel instantly anywhere in the Universe. They have seven active members that serve on the Spiritual Hierarchy. They have a vibrational energy that is much higher than ours and it's closer to the 8th Dimensions around 7.98.

Like the other species they walked a certain path back to the Source. They are considered to be The Ancient Lords of Light. Though they have dwindled in numbers they are still highly respected members of the Council. They hold vast knowledge and experience from all their time evolving.

The next oldest of the extraterrestrial races is the Pleiadians. They have been exploring space for the past 2 billion years. Some of the Sirians and all of the Pleiadians became the Guardians of the Light. The Pleiadians often appear as Angelic beings to humanity and the other younger races. They are often referred to as "shining ones" in the more ancient human texts. There are seven distinct star systems within the Pleiades and those systems make up the seven ruling houses. The systems and houses are An, Kera, Sera, I'la, Am, Nu and Is. Each of those houses has a head who governs the actions within their systems. I will discuss each system and household in detail to illustrate what each represent. Below I have provided a chart that lists all the systems and houses along with their heads.

The Pleiadians

Diagram 2

Pleiadian Systems and Households	The Heads of the Houses
An	Sananda
Kerah	Rah
Sara	Sarah
I'La	Aluna
Am	Amun
Nu	Numan
Is	Isis and Osiris

These systems and houses all share their technologies and cultural influences. Here some of the important things to know about the Pleiades.

- All the systems and houses share the same technologies. It is organic and silicon based. They utilize crystals to power and create their cities and starships
- They are related to the "seven heavens" in most ancient texts
- They appear to humans and the other younger species with wings of Light and a raiment
- They are composed of energy
- They are the servants of the Light and help younger species find their way back to the Source
- They vibrate between 7.5 and 7.8 frequencies

The greatest influence the Pleiadians have had on our Galaxy is the Ashtar Command. It was created during the great Draconian War over 100 million years ago. Since that time, it has evolved into the Galactic Federation of Planets. They will send envoys to the younger species during times of great transitions in consciousness. The seven houses are all represented on the Spiritual Hierarchy. Usually the head of the household or another member will serve on the various councils.

The Lyrans

The Lyrans are the next of the Ancient races. Originally, they had very little to do with humanity, but in the past fifty million years they have become more involved with this sector of the Galaxy. Presently, they rarely appear to Humanity anymore, but when they when they do make an appearance, they are very tall and lithe with pointed ears and eyebrows. Like the other ancient races, they are mostly composed of energy. Their home planet is much like Earth with 70% water and 30% land mass. Unlike the Earth they are in complete harmony with nature. Some important things to remember about Lyrans are:

- They are Immortal
- They were actively involved with Humanity up to 3,000 years ago
- Their ships are organic and look like gigantic whales in space
- They vibrate between 7.25 to 7.3 frequency

They observe humanity but they rarely take an active involvement in what is taking place in our world. They feel that our species must learn to resolve the imbalances They are generally neutral to what happens to humanity. They have seats on most of the councils.

The Annu& Naki

The last of the Ancient Ones is the Annu' Naki. They are actually offshoots of the Pleiadians. They decided to follow the dark ways during the onset of the Great Draconian War. They are considered the Lords of Chaos. Some important things to remember about this species are:

- They directly interact with humanity on a regular basis
- They are highly skilled at telepathic communication to manipulate the masses and individuals
- They do whatever it takes to create chaos on our planet
- They utilize organic technology like the ancients but it requires a living sacrifice to function

They serve on several councils in the Hierarchy. They should be avoided at all costs whenever possible.

The Elder Races

Arcturans	Orallens	Col'Notaros	Zeta Reticulans	Lizarians

The next five extraterrestrial races are known as the Elder Races. Like the Ancient Races they serve on either the Light or the Dark areas of Council. They have been space faring between fifty million and five million years. They are more actively involved with the younger races. These extraterrestrials are (1) The Arcturans, (2) The Orallens, (3) The Col'Notaros, (4) The Zeta Reticulans, and (5) The Lizarians. They all serve on the Councils of the Spiritual Hierarchy.

The Arcturians

The Arcturians are the oldest of the Elder races. They began space faring about 5 million years ago. Their government is ruled by a technocracy. They value logic and science above all things. Their Science is based upon being in balance with nature. They have had the basics of organic technology for about 1 million years. Some important things to know about the Arcturians are:

- Planetary system is in the Arturus Constellation
- Their home planet is known Articulan
- They are physically very tall sitting well over 30 feet and have a large conical Cranium
- They are highly advanced technologically
- They are friendly towards the younger races
- They vibrate at a 6.75 frequency

An aspect of their large Cranium has granted them highly developed mental abilities. In fact their technology is driven by mind power. They are now the primary monitors of the Ascension Gene throughout the galaxy.

The Orions: Orallens and Col&Notaros

The "Light" Orions: The Orallens

The Orions are the next of the Elder races. They were split between the forces of Light and Darkness during the Great War. Even though they were originally the same species they have become two very distinct races. The Pleiadians claimed dominion over the Orallens at the end of the Great War. They were named the Light Orion's. The Orallens have been space faring for the past 2.5 million years. Some of the important things to remember about the Orallens are:

- Their homeworld is known as Oralla
- They are highly evolved spiritually and technologically
- They host the Council of the Twenty-Four for the Spiritual Hierarchy
- They have organic technology in their cities and starships
- They are humanoid in appearance and stand about 6-10 meters
- They have little hair and have large pronounced eyes
- They are mostly healers and guardians
- They have 12 members that rotate in service on the Councils

The Orallens are friendly towards the younger species but they do not currently like the way humanity is heading.

The Col'Notaros: The Dark Orions

The other Orion species is called the Col' Notaros. They are known as the Dark Orions. At the end of the Great Draconian War, the Annu'Naki took these Orions to do with as they will. They completely perverted and warped this race so much so that they no longer even share genetic codes with their former race. They were trained to be the forerunners and warriors of Darkness. Some important things to remember about them are:

- They used to be the same species as the Orallens but were altered after the Great War
- Their home world is known as Col' Notaur and it is on the left side of Orion's Belt
- Their home planet has been completely stripped of all its natural resources
- They are extremely aggressive and predatory
- They enjoy manipulating the younger species to lead them towards the path of Darkness

The Dark Orions are heavily involved with the governments of our world. They are tipping the scales of balance on this planet and something must be done about it. Part of what must take place in the Aquarian Age is a restoration of balance within and in the outer world as well.

The Zeta Reticulans

The Zeta Reticulans are the next species of the elders. They have been spacefaring for about 1 million years. They have only come to our sector of the galaxy in past 2000 years. Here are some important things to remember about this race.

- They are the most commonly seen species in modern times
- Their species is dying and they are looking for new species to reinvigorate their genetic pool
- They evolved from insectoids
- They are neutral observers on Council though they have a tendency to side with Chaos
- They are completely devoid of emotions

The Zetas have an arrangement with several governments on this planet to perform experiments on the population in exchange for technology.

The Lizarians

The Lizarians are the last of the Elder extraterrestrial races. They are also known as the Reptilians. The Lizarians were genetically enhanced by the Annu'Naki about 10 millions years ago. They are considered to be the most deadly and dangerous alien race in the Galaxy. They are reptilian in nature. Physically they stand approximately six to seven meters tall. They are highly trained warriors and assassins. Some important things to know about the Lizarians are

- They are the front lines for the dark forces
- They can change their shape and appear like any of the other species
- They have unique smells probably stemming from their earlier evolution
- Their starships are disc shaped
- They have been space-faring for 350,000 years

They are considered to be extremely dangerous and are highly intelligent. Be very careful when you encounter one in your journeys.

The Spiritual Hierarchy

All of the extraterrestrial races mentioned in the above sections of this chapter are part of the Spiritual Hierarchy. The hierarchy is made up of various levels of councils. As shown in the above diagram, it begins with the Source. The Source is the source of all life and balance in the Universe. Following this down from the Source you come to the Council of the One. It consists of all space faring races. The other Councils branch out from this Council in the manner shown in the above diagram. Most of the lower Councils consist of twelve members and have specific areas to monitor. For each of the council's I have bulleted their primary functions to make it easier to understand what they do.

There are thirteen councils in all and the diagram above illustrates how they flow. All the councils stem from the Source of All Life. The Source is neither male nor female, good nor evil it just is. It flows through everything and all the dimensions of this Universe. It is what we are all evolving towards in spirit. Our souls are merely tiny fragments of this Source. The primary function of the Source is to maintain balance with all life in the Universe.

The Council of the One

The Council the One is the closest to the Source. It is made up of 162 members from all of the space-faring Extraterrestrial Races. They have come from both sides of the Duality in the Universe. Together they create a perfect symmetry of balance. Their primary functions are as follows:

- Hear all cases that cannot be resolved in the lower councils
- Ensure that balance is maintained throughout the Universe
- Enacting the Will of the Source
- All of the Ancient and Elder Races serve on this Council plus any representatives of the other space faring races

All of the decisions and information on balance are filtered down from here to the other councils. This Council meets biannually unless there is a major emergency. I have served on this Council for many lifetimes.

The Council of the Twenty-four

From the Council of the One we move into the the Council of the Twenty-Four. This Council consists of 12 members on the side of Light and Order and 12 members from the side of Chaos and Darkness. There are two members from each of the nine extraterrestrial races plus three sets from the younger space faring species. This Council usually meets once a month. Their primary functions are:

- Hear the cases that could not be resolved in the lower councils
- Enact and empower the wishes of the Council of the One coming from the Source
- Ensure and maintain balance in the Universe
- All of the major extraterrestrial races are represented on this Council

This council is closely involved with the younger species including humanity. The members of this council are answerable to the Council of the One.

The Council of Light and Order

There are two councils under the Council of the Twenty-Four. They are the Council of Light and Order and the Council of Darkness and Chaos. They both consist of twelve members and they maintain the balance in the Universe. The Council of Light's primary functions are:

- Ensure the ongoing nature of order in the Universe
- Empower those individuals they deem appropriate to be the vehicles of order
- Manage the enforcers of the Light known as the "Melcheizeldek Order"
- Gather all information from the lower councils and determine if assistance is needed
- Enforce the Will of the Source and higher Councils
- This Council is directly involved with humanity

I have served on this Council for many lifetimes. They take whatever means necessary to maintain balance on the Earth and the Universe.

The Council of Darkness and Chaos

The Council of Darkness and Chaos is made up of the major extraterrestrial races that serve darkness and chaos. There are twelve members on this council. Some of the major functions of this council are as follows:

- Ensure the ongoing nature of Chaos to promote Evolution of younger species
- Manipulate the younger species to provide misinformation to confuse the "Truth"
- Manage the enforcers of Chaos known as the Lords of Chaos
- Gather all information from the lower councils to determine how best to serve Chaos
- This council is directly involved with humanity
- They are not hindered by oaths of non-interference and harmlessness

Through the Lords of Chaos, they have a strong influence over the powers that are on this planet. They have created a strong imbalance between nature and humanity on Earth.

The Council of Karma

The Council of Karma is the next part of the hierarchy. It is made up of Twelve members of the E.T.'s that serve the Light. The members consist of one Pleiadian, two Arcturians, two Orallens, and seven members of the younger species including humanity. The primary functions of this Council are as follows:

- To judge all beings in the Universe on the basis of the lessons they must learn in specific lifetimes
- Enforce the Laws of Karma and Dharma in the Universe
- They are Keepers of the Akashic Records

This council is very involved with the human race. This council is answerable to the Council of Light and Order.

The Council of the Priesthood

This council is made up of twelve members. It usually consists of six priests and six priestesses but the number can vary depending on certain circumstances. They usually come from different worlds throughout the known Universe. The primary functions of this council are as follows:

- Provide assistance and guidance to initiates of the priestly orders
- Stand in judgement over individuals who have done great wrongs against other species

This council is answerable to the Council of Light and Order. Their primary interest is in the younger species.

The Council of Light Masters and Healers

This council is also known as the Council of Lightworkers and Healers. There are twelve members that serve on this council. The Pleiadian, Archangel Raphael, and the Lyran, Achiel co-chair this council. The council also consists of three more Pleiadians and three Orallens. The rest are rotating and come from the various younger species. The primary functions are as follows:

- Monitor and assist all Lightworkers and healers across the galaxy
- Monitor all information that is released through spiritual means to the younger species
- This council meets bi weekly
- They are answerable to the Council of Light and Order

I have served on this Council for many lifetimes.

The Council of Interspecies Relations

The next part of the hierarchy is known as the Council of Interspecies Relations. This council represents the interests of all the younger species that have achieved interstellar travel. Currently there are fifty-four members that serve on this council. There are two members from every system that has the ability to travel the stars. They come from both sides the Light and Dark. Their primary functions are as follows:

- Ensure balance is maintained between Chaos and Order
- Ensure the peace and balance between the younger species

They are not directly involved with humanity yet. However, they do pay attention to how things are playing out on this planet.

The Council on Human Affairs

The Council on Human Affairs consists of twelve members. It is made up of two Pleiadians, one Sirian, one Lyran, three Annu'Naki, one Arctuiran, one Zeta Reticulan, one Lizarian, one Orallen, and one Col" Notaroan. The primary functions of this Council are:

- Monitor all affairs of the human race
- Implement actions to ensure balance within the human population on the planet Earth
- Monitor the progress of the ascension gene on the planet
- Monitor all races that are directly involved with the human race
- Enforce the "Right to Choose" edict for this sector of the galaxy

All members of this council are actively involved with planet Earth and Humanity. They monitor all avenues of information on the planet. The "Right to Choose" Edict was passed after humanity was freed from slavery under the rule of the Annu'Naki several hundred thousand years ago. This Edict provides humanity with the right to choose how they wish to return to the Source. I serve on this council.

The Council of Galactic Balance

The Council of Galactic Balance is the next part of the Spiritual Hierarchy. There are twelve members that serve on this council, six on the side of Order and six on the side of Chaos. The primary functions of this council are:

- Ensure the maintenance of balance between the forces of order and chaos
- Monitor the younger races to ensure balance is maintained

This council has taken particular interest in the planet Earth. This interest is due to the incredible imbalances we are facing in our world today.

The Council of Chaotic Evolution and Ascension

The Council of Chaotic Evolution is the next part of the Spiritual Hierarchy. This council consists of twelve members. Their primary functions are:

- Monitor the processes of evolution in the younger species
- Manipulate through cataclysmic events which encourage the process of evolution
- Cull the younger species of unnecessary genetic material

This council answers to the Council of Chaos and Darkness and the Council of Light and Order. They are heavily involved with humanity.

The Council of Fear and Control

The Council of Fear and Control is a 12-member council. All of its members follow Chaos and Darkness. Their primary functions are as follows:

- Use Blood Magic to manipulate and control the younger species
- Promote the disempowerment of specific sub groups in a population using fear and manipulation

This council is excessively involved on the planet Earth. They are the primary creators of fear, hatred, and intolerance on this planet. They do this manipulation both directly and indirectly with human beings.

The Council of the Dark Ways

The Council of the Dark Ways is the last of the Councils on the Spiritual Hierarchy. It has twelve members that all serve Chaos and Darkness. Their primary functions are as follows:

- Promote corruption and pain in all of the younger species
- Promote through manipulation the importance of fame and power

This council has been heavily involved with humanity for a millenia. Their control over the human population has dramatically increased in the past 30 years.

Conclusion

In this chapter, I discussed the 9 major extraterrestrial races and the spiritual hierarchy. Extraterrestrials have been visiting the planet Earth for many millions of years. In fact, most human cultures refer to them as gods or angels. These alien races are divided into two distinct age groups the Ancients and the Elders. The only real difference between them is the number of years they have been traveling space and their connectedness to the Source. All of them serve in some capacity on the Spiritual Hierarchy. The hierarchy has all of its authority from the Source of all Life. There are 13 councils that exist as part of the hierarchy. These councils are important because they guide the population of this planet towards balance and harmony. Indeed, this equilibrium will help us in achieving what is needed during this transition time.

Love and Laughter

Shakespeare wrote: "Love is a many splendid thing" These words are some of the truest words ever written. Though they are meant for romantic love, they can be applied to the essence of love as well. Love is the most wonderful and powerful gift we have. Yet so many people squander this gift over petty beliefs of superiority or false truths taken from various pieces of culture. The transition period we are in now marks these occurrences across the globe. There is always some group causing problems based upon hatred because someone is of a different color skin, religion, gender or sexual orientation. These issues all stem from fear and are not based on love. When love is flowing in your heart it is simple to see the Divine Sparks in others.

Laughter is another key ingredient in this tumultuous period. It combines with love to create an awesome expression of joy and peace. Laughter is considered by many of my teachers to be one of the many paths to enlightenment. Laughter like love is a very powerful tool we can use to reject the negative energies that abound in the world around us. I have personally experienced the joys of laughter in my everyday life. Through it I have been able to rise above predicaments that others would have found daunting. I believe that laughter instills a transcendental state of being on the entire planet. My theory is if everyone on the planet laughs in the same instance the resulting cathartic event would release us all from the illusions of pain, suffering and deprivation. My dream is to one day make this a reality.

In this chapter, I will discuss what love is and the importance of it in our daily lives. My teachers taught me the nine aspects of love and how to affect them into everyday living. I will also share the importance of laughter in regards to your overall well-being. Finally, I will look at how both of these working in conjunction with each other can help you as the planet moves through this transition time. Love and laughter are the keys to a better way of life for everyone on this planet.

What is love?

What is love? Many scholars and theologians throughout the ages have pondered that question. Christian theologians even went so far as to classify love into three different categories: Eros, platonic and agape. Love is truly a very powerful force within this universe. It is difficult to classify and contain it within human comprehension. It simply is a part of all life in the Universe. The conditions you have placed on yourselves and others are simply misguided conceptions on the incomprehensible. Love is greater than any one person, Nation or world. This section is about love. My teachers for this section were Jesus, the Buddha, and the Archangel Gabriel. They clarified many things about love for me. They taught me how to live my life in love. Non-judgmental pure love for all things in this Universe.

To begin, I will discuss some of the common misconceptions you might have about love. You must remember that love is an emotion and it exists primarily in the fifth chakra near the heart. Love is a feeling and it is not a thought. Many people confuse feelings for thoughts where love is concerned. For example, many people will say or think to themselves or others: "I think I love this person." This thinking is inaccurate because love is illogical and is entirely based on emotions. You cannot think you love somebody or something because it is just there. Thinking about love will only get your Ego involved in something where it should not be. Trying to think about an emotion is like trying to fish in the sand. It is not a possibility. Love is irrational and truly based on feelings from your heart. Of course, you will love all things because all things come from the Source.

The notion that love is romantic is another direction created by artists and writers of the Renaissance Era. While their concepts are beautiful and can lead to true love, they are not real. Romantic love is about eroticism and chemical reactions in the body. Whenever you find someone attractive you "think" you might have found love with that person. All you are really experiencing is a rush of endorphins from the brain to the body. This chemical reaction has nothing to do with true love. The Christian theologians called this erotic love and it is purely physical. My teachers agreed that it is purely physical and it has nothing to do with love. This physical attraction casts many Illusions and can lead people to place conditions and expectations upon one another.

Indeed, these conditions lead us to judge others unfairly through misguided expectations. These expectations are usually created in your early learning process growing up. They can also be created and held over from past lives which creates a never-ending cycle of fear and loveless relationships. Whenever you limit another by placing conditions on your love for them you are also limiting yourself. When we block people off from the love that exists between two divine sparks, we are jeopardizing ourselves and everything else on the planet.

Opening ourselves up to the love in our hearts allows us to enter new vistas of connectedness to the world around us. Not only will it connect you with others but it will bring you closer to the Source of All Life as well. Love is a good feeling inside your heart chakra. Not only is it important to love others but it is equally important to love yourself. Loving yourself is tantamount to opening yourself up to the larger **Love** of the Universe. I always ask people how often they look in the mirror and say to themselves "I love you." I am not talking about narcissism where you constantly look at your reflection but every once in a while, looking in a mirror and staring in your eyes and saying "I love you." When you do this, it will help break down the fears and Illusions you have created around your image and yourself. It will open you up to unconditional love.

Exercise

1. For one week use a mirror to look into your eyes and say "I love you." Do this once a day. Watch the changes that happen to your entire being and how you relate to others.

The Nine Aspects of Love

My teachers shared some things that will help you to learn about love and how to experience it in your daily life. These are called the Nine Aspects of Love. These aspects are reception, honesty, forgiveness, compassion, affectionate expression, joy, gratitude, fearlessness and being yourself. When these are combined, they help you to access the infinite stores of love within yourself and the Universe. In this section, I will elaborate on each of these areas and explain how they can benefit your daily living. At the end of the section there are some exercises to help you integrate them into your lives.

The first aspect of love is to be receptive to the love around you. It is sometimes difficult to see love in our lives because we feel we have been abused or hurt by others. However, when you open your heart to receive the love in your world you will find that you are filled to overflowing with loving energy. This energy will allow you to heal your wounds and help you to be there for others. To be receptive it is vitally important to open your Heart Chakra. In order to access the love in your life, open your Heart Chakra and the Christ Consciousness Chakra. It will also help you to visualize yourself with a lotus flower in your Heart Chakra opening up to the light of Love. After doing this meditation, you will feel your heart overflowing with love. Being receptive to love is the first aspect and you must relearn how to feel the love in your life.

The next aspect of Love is honesty. This means you must be fiercely honest with yourself and others. It is much better to tell the truth about all things within yourself and the relationship you share with others. Not only will it help you to open your heart but it will create healthy relationships for you. When you acknowledge all the characteristics of yourself you can begin to create a better way to exist in this world. We all have some good, bad, and ugly things within ourselves because we are all aspects of the Source. Once you have learned to love all of those things about yourself, it will help you to express yourself fully to others.

Forgiveness is the next Aspect of Love. Forgiveness is not always easy but can be accomplished. When somebody or even yourself does something against you it is normal to get angry, but it is difficult to forgive. It also helps to be able to forgive yourself. It frees up the energy held in the Heart Chakra. Whenever we feel resentment towards someone from a past transgression it can block the energy flows in your body known as the *Chi*. When the *Chi* is blocked it can cause health problems and make it difficult for you to associate with people around you. It can prevent you from accessing the Source which further inhibits your ability to live a rich full life.

Compassion is the next Aspect of Love. It is important because it will open your heart chakra up to empathy for others. It will open new vistas for understanding yourself and others. Becoming compassionate with your own shortfalls as a human being will help you to become more sympathetic to others around you. Learning to love yourself for all your triumphs and sufferings will open the gates of Love in Your Heart. It will also open the bigger gateway to service for others which is a major part of the healing we need in this Aquarian Age.

Expressing your affection of Love is the next Aspect that helps it open your heart to unconditional love. Affection is expressing your feelings of love towards another through physical, emotional and spiritual intimacy. Affection of your feelings is a very normal human behavior and it also enhances your connectedness to others. Kissing, hugging, touching and all other forms of intimacy are all part of the expression of your affection for others. (This does not mean inappropriate touching such as private areas of the human body like the buttocks or genital area). Whenever you make love with another person you are connecting with that person on a very deep level and the connection you share with each other will be with you forever. For this reason, anonymous sex with others is not the best idea unless you are fully prepared for the burden that it will place on your heart. You will forever remain attached to that person even when your mind forgets, your heart will always remember. Beyond the sexual intimacy of affection just the basic hugging and kissing and touching among those are those you care about is vital to opening your heart chakra to unconditional Love. As a species, human beings need to be touched daily by each other. An example of this occurred during the Chechneyan War. There were thousands of orphaned infants left after the devastation and many of them were deprived of the human touch for days or weeks. Without the touch most of those infants died and were non-responsive. This example helps to illustrate the vital importance of affection and touch in our feeling the unconditional Love.

Another Aspect of unconditional Love is Joy. It comes from deep inside your heart chakra and it makes you feel like laughing and singing. Joy comes from the overflowing feeling of bliss in your Heart Chakra. Bliss occurs when you fully open your heart to the abundance of Love around you. When Joy is fully active in your heart energies it can actually warm your body. To help facilitate the activation of joy in your life, open your heart chakra. Once you have mastered this by doing it several times a week you will begin to feel the easiness of joy in love.

The next Aspect of Love is gratitude. Being thankful for the things you do have in your everyday life. For instance, you can be grateful for the roof over your head or the food on your table. You can also be glad to be alive and have good friends and family. Creating a list of things, you are grateful for in your life can help you to open your heart in gratitude towards Love. Keeping a daily list can also help in keeping depression and anxiety at bay. With gratitude towards all things in your life you have learned an important Aspect of Love.

Being fearless is another Aspect of Love. This means you should be willing to allow the full expression of love in your life. It is through fear that we prevent the existence of love to be present in our world. Unconditional Love can be frightening because you might be afraid you will get hurt or worse. However, when you approach Love from a place of fearlessness it becomes much easier to cope with these barriers. An exercise that helps you to conquer your fears about love is to explore your fears by writing them down in a journal. By writing your fears down you actually give less power to them because you become more conscious of them. You can also explore how you have created barriers to others through intolerance and hatred in your life. These feelings are also created out of fear and ignorance about other people. Fear can impede your growth and stop your unconditional acceptance of all life in the Universe. Once you have learned to take back your power in regards to Love by disempowering the fear in your heart you have mastered another Aspect of Love.

All of these aspects come together in the fulfillment of the final aspect which is being yourself at all times. Through the application of the above aspects of love you will find it easier to be who you truly are. When you are able to be your true self you open the door for your Higher Self to enter your life. The higher self is that expression of the Divine Spark Within. This process can be difficult because many people are conditioned to live their lives behind mask of illusions. Once you are expressing your true self these things disappear because it will become unnecessary to live in a lie while living in Love.

All nine aspects can be worked on simultaneously or individually to create an open heart. My personal experiences with learning these Aspects have been through trial and error. It has made me a better person. It took me many years to grasp my emotions and feel the loving Bliss in my heart. When I was younger, I took things more personally and invoked the anger of my warrior spirit. With patience and love, I learned how to love myself and others through unconditional love. From these Aspects, I have learned how to transmute the negativity that sometimes flows into my life into a positive loving energy.

Unconditional love will transform your life. Once you have mastered yourself, it can bestow upon you all the truly beautiful things in life. By practicing the lessons of the Nine Aspects of love you can open yourself up to new vistas of possibilities. My own personal experience with unconditional love has aided me in becoming what I am today. Through love you can conquer all. Below I have provided some exercises of Nine Aspects of Love to help you master yourself and the understanding of unconditional love.

Exercise

1. Begin by keeping a journal on all your personal experiences with unconditional love
2. Work through all nine aspects individually and together on a daily basis. Write in journal, everything you are experiencing. How can you open yourself up so you can have more love in your life?
3. Practice meditating on the Heart Chakra to open the door for greater love in your life.
4. Make a daily gratitude list for one week.
5. Write down in your Journal all the fears you have surrounding love of yourself and others. How can you alter these fears to empower yourself in love?
6. **Be Yourself!**

Laughter: The Doorway that Bursts Open

Have you ever felt your laughter bubbling up from inside you? Have you ever laughed for no apparent reason? If you answered yes to either of these then you will truly appreciate what I have to say in this section. Laughter is the ultimate expression of Joy which is why it goes along with unconditional love. There are several physical and spiritual benefits of laughter. These benefits help us to fully express unconditional love in our lives. Combined they create the two most powerful tools in the Aquarian Age.

Laughter has three primary physical benefits:

1. endorphins: the natural balancer
2. relaxation for the entire body, and
3. cathartic release.

The body is an amazing machine that is designed to compensate for any physical imbalances within it. For instance, sweating is the body's way to help regulate its ambient temperature. Laughter too works in this manner. It helps relieve the tension created by various stressors in your life. A *stressor* is anything in the in the environment that causes stress (Random House Unabridged Dictionary, 1993, page 1882). For example, you may have just moved and it makes your neck and shoulders very tight. By laughing you release multiple endorphins into your body causing your muscles to relax. It always helps to have people in your life that make you laugh because they help to lighten the load. Endorphins are hormones released by the body in times of stress. They are similar to opiates produced exclusively in the human body. They act as natural equalizers to help you maintain balance. Therefore, with a little laughter you can take away the tension the stressor has caused in your life.

The next physical benefit of laughter is it makes the internal organs of the body function better when the endorphins are released. It is important to laugh because it helps to release the toxins held in various organs. It can help to strengthen and tone your muscles so you can live a happier and healthier life. Of course, the kind of laughter needed here is what I call the "throw your head back" and belly laugh. Once this is accomplished you should feel more relaxed about any situation. After your entire body relaxes you become more clear mentally and emotionally. It can help you open up to higher vistas of understanding. Your entire body relaxes after a good laugh and your mind becomes clear and focused.

The final physical benefit of laughter is cathartic release. Like crying laughter is considered to be a tool used to release pent up emotion. This benefit ties in with the other two benefits because it is through cathartic laughter that we experience a deep internal massage. All the organs experience a flow of endorphins into the entire body. Combined they can help everyone relax and reach their Highest Potential.

Beyond the physical benefits of laughter there are spiritual ones as well. When we laugh we open ourselves to a new paradigm of being or bliss. Laughter is an outward expression of joy. It is an excellent defense against negative energy and with cathartic laughter you can get in touch with your Higher Self. These three things are the major benefits of laughter in your spiritual expression.

The new paradigm that is created starts with laughter as an outward expression of the joy you feel in your heart. When your Heart Chakra opens to feel the full amount of love in your life you will experience Joy. This feeling always leads to laughter. My grandmother used to say laughter is caused by "the Angels tickling your ribs." Of course, this may well be true but it is an outward manifestation of the Source in your life. Do not be frightened if you experience random moments of laughter for no apparent reason. This reaction is normal when you fully open your heart chakra to allow bliss in your life.

The next spiritual benefit of laughter is it creates a natural barrier within your mind against negativity. Negativity destroys our greatest intentions unless we can learn to lighten ourselves and laugh with abandon. The negativity will just flow around the field of love you have created for yourself. Taking yourself less seriously will help tremendously with restoring your balance with the forces of love and life.

The last way that laughter benefits you spiritually is by providing a deep emotional release in the form of cathartic laughter. Not only will it help you physically but it will release all the pain and sorrow you have held onto from your past. Once you have accomplished this you will be more open to experiencing love in your life. Below I have provided some exercises to help you integrate laughter into your daily life.

Exercise

1. Meditate on opening your Heart Chakra and allowing love and laughter into your life.
2. **Laugh Daily!**
3. Find a group of friends with whom you can laugh and play at the many things, life throws at you.

Conclusion

Love in the Aquarian Age is the most important thing. Without it we cannot hope to fulfill humanity's greatest destiny. We are the bearers of choice in this galaxy and it is through love that we can achieve a reconnection to the Source of All Life. By proactively engaging in a daily effort to fully live in the Nine Aspects of Love we can open our hearts to the needs of the entire planet. Going hand-in-hand in love is the ability to laugh. It is the ultimate expression of joy throughout our Universe. One of my favorite quotes sums it up very well. "Laugh often, Love much and live fully…" I leave these words to you as a daily mantra. Be Blessed.

Glossary

Achiel: He is Lyran an ancient race and can appear to be elfin in nature. He is one of the co-chairs of the Council of Light Masters and Healers. He teaches many of the younger races races the importance of being in tune with the natural world.

Advanced Journeyman: Within the Psychic Trinity, this is the fifth stage of psychic development. People at this Stage of Development have had several years of experience and training with their gifts. Therefore, their gifts are more honed than the levels below them but not quite as acute as the master or adept stages.

Adept: Within the Psychic Trinity this is the Seventh Stage of Psychic Development. People at this Stage of Development have had many years of experience utilizing their gifts and service to the larger community. Even though a person at this level will continue to evolve their gifts, this is the highest stage of experience anyone can obtain.

Affection: This is one of the Nine Aspects of Love. It is expressed through physical intimacy with those that you love. This can take the form of hugging, kissing, holding hands, massaging or love making.

Through that you can build deeper and more profound relationships within your soul family or group.

Agape: This is the highest form of love that Christian theologians believe Humanity can attain. It refers to Divine love rather than conditional love.

Akashic Hall of Records: This is the place in The Fifth Dimension where all the past lives of every soul are stored for review. These are also known as the Akashic Records. When you die you usually go here to review the lessons you learned during each life and connect to the lifetimes that affected the one most recently departed. You may visit the hall at any time by astral projection.

Akashic Records: See the Akashic Hall of Records.

Aluna: is the head of the House of I'Lai in the Pleiadian constellation.

AM: Is one of the seven major houses and planetary systems in the Pleiadian constellation.

Amun: Is the head of the house of AM in the Pleiadian constellation.

AN: is one of the seven major houses in planetary systems of the Pleiadian constellation.

Ancient Races: The extraterrestrial races that have been traveling the stars for billions of years. They are the Sirians, the Pleiadians, the Lryans, and the Anun' Naki.

Angel: They are the guardians and protectors of the younger races. They were originally Pleiadian but have grown to include some of the other ancient and elder races. They all vibrate at a 6.21 pattern but can lower their vibration to be seen by the younger races. Due to their higher frequency the younger races usually perceive them as having wings.

Apprentice: Within the Psychic Trinity this is the Third Stage of Psychic Development. At this stage people about have about a year or two of training and practice with their gifts. While they have been practicing with their gifts longer than a beginner or novices they still have a long disciplined road of experience and practice ahead of them.

Aquarian Age: This is the present Age of the planet Earth and all of humanity. It represents freedom and equality for all and in every facet of life. The ages are based upon the twelve spoked wheel in western astrology but they move backwards and not forwards. Periods between the various Ages are called transition periods and almost are always fraught with social environmental unrest.

Aquarius: is one of the twelve signs in Western Astrology. This sign is frequently associated with electricity, freedom of expression, universal truths, the element of Air, the intellect and the planet Uranus.

Archangel: They are Pleiadians that vibrate at a higher frequency than regular Angels Humans on the planet Earth are familiar with 12 archangels that have visited this place in the past. The four most commonly known archangels are Archangel Michael, Archangel Gabriel, Archangel Raphael, and Archangel Uriel. They are the commanders of the various areas of the Pleiadian hierarchy and they serve as counselors or chairs at various councils of the spiritual hierarchy.

Archangel Gabriel: One of the four most commonly seen archangels in the modern times. She is also known as the Messenger of God. Within the spiritual hierarchy she serves on several councils. She is a Pleiadian in origin and it is believed that she is several billion years old. Her true form is purely energetic though she can appear to the younger species in times of great need. For example, she appeared to the Virgin Mary and Muhammad. When she does appear to the younger race's she is over 30 ft tall with beautiful wings and intensely red hair.

Archangel Michael: One of the four most commonly seen Archangels in modern times. Within the spiritual hierarchy he is the chair of the Council of Light and Order. He is the head of the Melcheizeldek Order. He is a Pleiadian in origin and it is believed that he is one of the oldest archangels. He played a major role in the defeat of the Dark Forces during the Great Dragon War. He is a purely energetic being but will appear before a chosen individual of the younger races in times of great need. When he does appear he will be seen as a being over 50 ft tall with intense violet eyes with long flowing ebony colored hair. He is the bearer of one of the Swords of Heaven. He is known as the commander of all Angelic forces.

Archangel Raphael: One of the four most commonly seen Archangels in modern times. Within the spiritual hierarchy he is the co-chair the Council of The Light Masters and Healers. He is commonly seen by people that are very ill and need intense healing. He works closely with healers like doctors and nurses Therapists and social workers. When he does appear before his charge's he is very tall standing over 50 feet with long flowing auburn hair and intense green eyes. He is the bearer of one of the swords of Heaven which appears as a rod.

Archangel Uriel: One of the four most commonly known Archangels in modern times. He rarely appears before the younger races.

Arcturians: are the oldest of the Elder extraterrestrial races. They begin traveling in space about 5 million years ago. They are very logical and value technology above all others all things. They stand over 30 ft tall and have a large cranium. They have extremely advanced psychic abilities and power they spaceships as cities by using their mind.

Arcturus: is the Home Star for the Arcturians. From the night sky on the planet Earth this star is usually seen in the springtime. It is the alpha star on the Bootes constellation also known as the herdsman. It is the fourth brightest star in the night sky. Arcturus is also known as "The Bear Watcher" since it follows Ursa Major around the night sky.

Aries: is the first sign in Western Astrology. It is commonly associated with passion, Independence, Innovation, the element of fire and the planet Mars.

Ascended Masters: are the teachers and guides that have reached a state of higher frequency. They have moved up the vibrational patterns in understanding and practice of the universal laws of Love and Life. They will sometimes appear to the younger races and times of evolutionary advancement.

Ashtar Command: The organization that is headed by Ashtar. It is made up of members of the various extraterrestrial and terrestrial species that agree before birth to assist in the Ascension process.

Astral Journey: is done during an astral projection. It refers to where you are going and what you are doing during these out of body experiences.

Astral Plane: This refers to the various levels one might experience during an astral projection. It also refers to the different dimensional frequencies that exists in the broader dimensions.

Astral Projection: This is the out of body experience that occurs for many people when their Spirit leaves its physical bonds for a short time. A silver cord maintains the spirits connectedness to the physical so that the individual soul can find its way back to its body.

Astrology: A system that is used to explain the cosmology of individual and global effects. Most ancient cultures have systems of astrology that related to their individual environments. In modern times there are several systems remaining from those times but the most prevalent are categorized into two distinct systems: Western and Eastern. All the modern systems have twelve distinct signs that are based upon the characteristics of certain animals from the outer environment. In reference to the ages there will be distinct qualities and Universal Truths that will be brought forth during these periods.

Aura: is the bioelectric field that surrounds the body. Everybody has a primary and secondary color in their energy fields.

Avatar: This is the Seventh Level of Psychic Development within the Psychic Trinity. They are individuals that can access all the others areas of psychic development. They are usually high- level souls.

Awareness: is what happens as the soul progresses up the evolutionary ladder of life. An aware individual can access various aspects of the higher knowing like it was second nature. They will see the world in a much fuller and truer light.

B

Base Chakra: is the energy center at the base of the spine. It is also known as the "Root" Chakra. It is commonly associated with survival issues. Its color is red.

Beginners: Within the Psychic Trinity this is the first Stage of Psychic Development. Individuals at this level will have flashes of whatever level their innate ability is functioning. With practice and discipline, they can reach higher stages of development.

Bible: The holy book of the Judeo-Christian world.

Bliss: This is the state that is obtained after opening the heart chakra to unconditional love in your life.

Blue: is one of the primary colors. It is associated with psychic ability, serenity, communication and peace.

Buddhism: is a philosophy and religion based on the teaching of the Buddha.

C

Cancer: is the fourth sign of Western Astrology. It is commonly associated with the crab, the element of water, emotional shields and feelings.

Capricorn: is the tenth sign of Western Astrology. It is associated with the goat, ambition, seriousness, the planet Saturn and mountains of the planet Earth.

Cataclysmic Events: are devastating events that usually results in the loss of many lives across the world. Some of the transition periods between the ages have seen this throughout the history of this planet. An example of this would be the great flood that was mentioned in many ancient texts.

Cathartic Release: is a release of emotions that causes the individual to let go of pent-up emotions being held inside the body. Crying and laughter are prime examples of methods of cathartic release.

Celts: are an Indo-Eurasian people around the second millennium BC. They had a highly advanced religion that honored various forms of marriages.

Centering: It is one of the fundamental pieces to have in building a positive spiritual base. If used correctly you will be balanced in all that you do. On a more mundane level if it is done properly you cannot be physically moved by any outside force.

Chakras: are the energy centers located along the spinal column in the human body. They vibrate at various frequencies and are attuned to various colors on the spectrum. When meditating on them you will see them swirling like a whirlpool in a clockwise or counterclockwise manner depending on your location on the planet.

Channel: is the Third Level of Psychic Development within the psychic trinity. Individuals at this level allow entities of a higher vibration to speak through them to others in the third dimension.

Cherubims: are Pleiadians. They are part of the Angelic host. Often associated with the seventh level of Heaven they have a very high vibrational frequency. In modern times artists have depicted them as His childlike entities with wings. They are always laughing singing and playing. In terms of the spiritual hierarchy they are part of the house and planetary system of Kera. They are extremely Advanced and most have already moved back to rejoin the Source. The ones that remain have taken of guardianship of members of the house and planetary system of AN. They are part of the Vanguard Group that has been sent to prepare the way for the New Age of Aquarius.

Christ/Buddha Consciousness: this is the advanced awareness imbued upon souls after reaching a certain level of conscious evolution. All Souls have this potential since everything originates from the Source.

Christianity: The religion and philosophy based upon the life and teachings of Jesus the Nazarene. The religion was greatly distorted in 333 A.D. leaving most of the knowledge of the Mysteries lost in antiquity.

Clairaudience: is one of the eight psychic aspects. It allows an individual to hear things from the Higher Dimensions. Usually it is a voice of a deceased relative or a spirit guide trying to warn of impending danger but it can also be solace or just a casual conversation.

Claircognizance: is one of the eight psychic aspects. It is a clear knowing. You experience it a deep knowing of something without any prior knowledge.

Clairempathy:. is one of the eight psychic aspects. It allows individuals the ability to sense other people/things emotions. The person has a deep connection to the emotional field.

Clairgustance: is one of the eight psychic aspects. It is clear tasting. One tastes something in the higher dimensions. It is usually associated with a deceased relative like an apple pie from grandma.

Clairsalience: is one of the eight psychic aspects. It means clear smelling. It allows the individual to smell things from a higher dimension.

Clairsentience: is one of eight psychic aspects. It is a physical knowing often called a "gut" feeling.

Clairtangency: is one of the eight psychic aspects. It is the ability to get a clear message about something through touching. It is also called psychometry.

Clairvoyance: is one of the eight psychic aspects. it is the ability to see into the higher dimensions.

Col'Notaos:are one of the Elder extraterrestrial races. They come from the Orion constellation. Originally, they were One race but they were taken after the Great Dragon War 5 million years ago by the Anunnaki to become Servants of the Dark Forces. They sit upon several of the council's associated with darkness and chaos.

Colors: are used in metaphysics for a variety of purposes. There are two significant things to remember regarding all colors. First the aura which surrounds the body and the chakra system along the spinal column are always a primary and a secondary color. Second it can influence the way people behave when they have an enclosed environment.

Community service: is service to the smaller community in a local environment. It involves assisting friends and families in need, volunteering at local organizations and assisting in the change of awareness in one's local environment. It is associated with a sixth level of the Soul.

Compassion: is one of the nine aspects of love. It entails a deep sympathy and pity for those that suffer. This sympathy encourages the individual to help through service to the larger community. It helps to open the heart chakra to greater expressions of unconditional love.

Constant Now: is that link in space and time which allows you access to the information you have learned from each lifetime so it can be utilized in the present moment.

Cosmic Consciousness: is the evolved awareness that is indicated by a fully awakened Divine Spark. The individual is able to access all areas of psychic ability and service. They are here to assist the planets in times of evolutionary advancement.

Council of Assisi: In 333 A.D., this Council was convened to discuss the direction of Christianity. Headed by Emperor Constantine, it was decided that many of the Great Mysteries presented by Jesus the Nazarene should be removed from the text of the Bible because it would threaten the sovereignty of the Catholic Church and the Holy Roman Empire.

Council of Chaos and Darkness: is one of the fourteen councils of the Spiritual Hierarchy. Its primary functions are to ensure the ongoing nature of chaos through the use of misinformation that manipulation. There are 12 members that serve on this council.

Council of Chaotic Evolution: is one of the fourteen councils of the Spiritual Hierarchy. Its primary function is to monitor the process of evolution in the younger species. They will in times of evolutionary leaps create cataclysmic events. There are 12 members that serve on this Council and they are answerable to the Council of Chaos and Darkness.

Council of Galactic Balance: is one of the fourteen councils of the Spiritual Hierarchy. Its primary function is to ensure that the balance between Chaos and Order or light and darkness are maintained. There are 24 members that serve on this Council.

Council of Human Affairs: is one of the fourteen councils of the Spiritual Hierarchy. Its primary functions are to monitor all affairs of humans throughout the Galaxy. There are 12 members on this Council.

Council of interspecies Relations: is one of the fourteen councils of the Spiritual Hierarchy. Its primary functions are to promote understanding and communication among the species in the Galaxy. There are two members from every species that have advanced enough to have Interstellar travel.

Council of Karma: is one of the fourteen councils of the Spiritual Hierarchy Its primary function is to judge all beings on the basis of things that they have done in their lifetime. They are the keepers of the akashic records. There are 12 members that serve on this Council.

Council of Light and Order: is one of the fourteen councils of the Spiritual Hierarchy. Its primary function is to ensure the basic order of the universe. Their enforcers are the Melcheizeldek Order. There are 12 members that serve on this Council.

Council of Light Masters and Healers: is one of the fourteen councils of the Spiritual Hierarchy. Its primary function is to guide all lightworkers and healers throughout the Universe. There are 12 members on this Council.

Council of the One: is one of the fourteen councils of the Spiritual Hierarchy.Its primary functions are to ensure the balance between Order and Chaos throughout the Galaxy and enacting the will of the Source. There are 162 members that serve on this Council.

Council of the Priesthood: is one of the fourteen councils of the Spiritual Hierarchy. Its primary functions are to provide assistance and guidance to initiates of priestly orders and to stand in judgment over individuals who have done great wrongs against any initiate. There are 12 members that serve on this Council.

The Council of Forty-Four: is one of the fourteen councils of the Spiritual Hierarchy. Its primary function is to maintain balance, between the opposing forces of the universe. There are 44 members that serve on this Council.

Creator: is one of the seven levels of psychic development. Individuals at this level of development can create many wonders of the world because they have direct access to the Source through their Divine Sparks.

Crown chakra: is one of the seven centers that run along the spinal column. This chakra is located at the top of the head and is violet in color.

Cultural Identity: is how an individual identify themselves to the norms and mores of a larger society.

D

Dark Forces: are those individuals or groups of Chaos and negativity.

Dark Ways: are the pathways and spirituality that follow a more negative and chaotic belief.

Déjà Vu: is the feeling or memory of having done something or been in a place before the present experience. It is often associated with the psychic aspect of precognition or Clairvoyance via dreams or visions.

Destiny: is what is supposed to happen for individuals when they are following the appropriate pathway.

Dharma: is the pathway that is the most moral and right according to universal laws.

Divine Spark: is the soul of the individual. It is that part of the source that separated itself from its origin to learn and understand the universe through varying experiences.

Dream Walker: is one of the abilities of an advanced visionary. They can walk into the dreams of others. They can manipulate people to do certain things for their dreams. This gift is very rare and they have very high ethical and moral standards.

Dream Walking: see Dream Walker.

ε

Earth Bonding Meditation: is one of the Advanced Grounding and Centering techniques that connects the individual with the planet Earth.

Earth Mudra Meditation: is one of the Advanced Grounding and Centering techniques that connects the individual to the planet through movement and breath.

Economy: is one of the five major social institutions. It primarily deals with the development of abundance and prosperity.

Education: is one of the five major social institutions. It primarily deals with the development of passing-down a society's beliefs and mores to the next generation.

Elder races: are those extraterrestrial races who have been traveling in space for millions of years. Those races are the Arcturians, the Orallens, the Col'Notaros, the Zeta Reticulans and the Lizarians.

Empathy: is one of the Pathic Abilities within the Psychic Trinity. It is the ability to feel what other others feel on the physical and emotional levels. At the more advanced levels an individual can make others feel any emotion they wish.

Endorphins: are hormones that maintain balances within the body system.

Energetic Fields: are the field surrounding all things in the universe. All energetic bodies have a specific vibration that help to determine what its function will be.

Entity: is anything outside of the individual that has expressed intelligence. It is usually in reference to beings from a higher vibrational frequency.

Equality: is one of the basic ideals that is coming forward in the Aquarian Age. It means that everybody will have the same rights and privileges in every area of the planet.

Equilibrium:.is that natural force which all things exist in this galaxy. It is a perfect balance between light and dark, Order & Chaos, positive or negative.

Eros: is the Christian theologian's explanation for erotic love between two people. It involves passion and lust and not actually is not true unconditional love.

Evolution: is the natural process of Life both spiritual and physical that affects everything in the universe. There are times throughout human evolutionary history that there have been Quantum leaps in the process that have created an even better way of being. The Aquarian Age is such a time.

Extraterrestrials: are any species or races that originated outside the planet Earth.

$\mathcal{F}$

Family: is one of the five major social institutions in a society.

Fearlessness: is one of the nine aspects of love. It means that an individual should not be afraid to fully express who and what they are in order to open your heart chakra to unconditional love.

Forgiveness: is one of the nine aspects of love. It means that an individual must be able to let go of past transgressions for themselves and others in order to open their heart chakra up to on conditional love.

$\mathcal{G}$

Galactic Core: is the center of the Galaxy it is also the center of all life in the galaxy.

Gemini: is one of the twelve Zodiac signs in astrology. It is associated with adaptability, intelligence, Duality, communication and the planet Mercury.

Gender: is the sex of an individual in any given lifetime. During the Age of Aquarius, the outmoded concepts of gender are being recreated to fit a more equal reality.

Ghosts: are entities from the fourth dimension. Usually they are disincarnate beings that have not moved on into the light.

Gifts: are those abilities granted to individuals to be of service to the larger community. They are often psychic or healing in nature and are considered to be the lower stages of the levels of psychic development.

Global Service: is associated with the seventh level of the Soul. Individuals at this level are here to guide the entire planet into a new way of being. Martin Luther King Jr and Gandhi are examples of the type of Global Service at this level.

God: is one of the manifestations of the Source that takes on a masculine aspect.

Goddess: is one of the manifestations of the Source that takes on a feminine aspect.

Government: is one of the five major social institutions of society. It deals primarily with maintenance of order in a society.

Grade School: is an aspect of the third level of soul development. It indicates that an individual soul at this level will be learning how to get along with the larger society. These individuals are usually very afraid of expressing their individuality and going against the status quo.

Gratitude: is one of the nine aspects of love. It means that by being thankful for all the wonderful things life has to offer you can open your heart chakra up to unconditional love.

Great Dragon War: Is the tumultuous events that occurred between the ancient extraterrestrial races between 100 million and 50 million years ago. The results of this war created a split into duality. Some races became the Lords of Order and Light and others became the Lords of Chaos and Darkness. After the war was over the Spiritual Hierarchy was created to maintain the balance between the two opposing forces.

Green: is one of the secondary colors of the spectrum. It is associated with the heart chakra, abundance, expansion and love.

Grounding: is the meditative technique that allows you to connect with the Earth and keep you connected to the reality around you.

Guardian Angels: are angels or deceased beings that are in the fourth or fifth Dimensions that aid members of the younger species throughout their lifetime. It is usually a contractual arrangement made with these entities before you were born.

Guardians: are witches of the highest order chosen at birth for their natural magical abilities. They are the keepers and protectors of various portals that connects to the other planes of existence. They are scattered throughout the planet and the Galaxy.

Guru: Is a spiritual teacher or advisor

ℋ

Heart Chakra: is the fifth chakra center along the spinal column. It is associated with love, abundance and expansion.

Hebrews: any group that can trace its origin from Abraham, Jacob or Isaac. They are one of the older surviving philosophical traditions that still have a highly sophisticated system of belief.

Higher Dimensions: any area of space and time that vibrates to a higher frequency from the third dimension. It is also associated with the higher planes.

Higher Planes: see Higher Dimensions.

Higher Self: is the ultimate expression of the Source of All Life that exists within all sentient beings. It is also referred to as the divine spark.

Hinduism: is the religious and philosophical system developed in India.

Honesty: is one of the nine aspects of love. It means that individuals who are open and candid with themselves and others will open their heart chakra to unconditional love.

Hormone: is a chemical produced in the body to helps maintain equilibrium.

Hypothalamus: the part of the brain in the human body contains the bridge for accessing the psychic ability and the higher dimensions.

I

I'la: is one of the great houses of the planetary system of the Pleiades. This group of ancients are part of a medical team and scientists within of the Ashtar Command.

Individual Level: is an aspect of the fifth level of Soul Development. Individuals at this level are obtaining their college degree Soul understanding. They fully express their individuality and know how to work for their own needs and the larger community or society. They become more involved in serving others who have less lifetime experience.

Intergalactic Classroom: is the classroom where individuals are taught how to prepare to enter in the Aquarian Age. It also prepares to join the Galactic Federation of Light.

Initiates: are those individuals that have completed certain levels of training within the metaphysical or magical community.

Intuition: is the ability to know things without an explanation of how it is known. It is the basis for development of psychic ability.

Intuitive Ability:.See intuition.

IS: is one of the great houses in planetary systems within the Pleiades. It is pronounced "ease." The angels from this household and system are often referred to as the guardian angels.

Istari: are the wizards and guardian witches that are here to serve and protect the human race.

Isis: is the title held by one of the heads of the great house IS in the Pleiades.

Islam: is the religious and philosophical belief based on the teachings of Muhammad.

J

Jesus the Nazarene: was a political and military leader during the first century A.D. He is also one of the bearers of a Cosmic Consciousness. His lessons of love and understanding for all were essentially wiped Away by the early Catholic Church. He is a Pleiadian and within the Ashtar Command is referred to as Master Sananda. He shares the position of head of the House of AN with the Lord Maitreya.

Journeyman: is the fourth stage of training and experience within the Seven Levels of Psychic Development. People at this stage have the ability to do some things without the assistance of a teacher or master.

Judaism: is the religious and philosophical system based on the teachings of Abraham, Moses and various other Prophets.

Judgement Day: In Christianity it is believed that their God will sit in judgement of all beings and weigh their sins. It is often associated with apocalyptic events.

K

Karma: is the lessons that one must learn during any given lifetime. It can carry over into other lifetimes if the lesson has not been learned.

KERA: is one of the great houses and planetary systems within the Pleiades. The head of the household is known by the title RE. They are often referred to as the Cherubim.

ℒ

Laughter: is the expression of laughing when one is filled with joy. Through it you can defend yourself against psychic attack and open your heart chakra to a greater expression of love in your life.

Leo: is one of the twelve zodiac signs. It is associated with the lion, adolescence, royalty, egomania, and the element of fire. It is closely associated with the Sun.

Libra: is one of the twelve zodiac signs. It is associated with the scales, law, balance, tyranny, beauty, high intellect, a balanced mind, the element of air and the Venus.

Lifetime: is the years a Soul exists in the third dimension.

Light: Is that part of the cosmic entities who follow the tenants and universal laws of order and positive energetics.

Light Masters: are those individuals that have attained the highest level of knowing down the path of life.

Lizarians: are one of the elder extraterrestrial races. They have been spacefaring for the past 150,000 years. They come from a reptilian background. They are considered highly aggressive and dangerous.

Lords of Chaos and Darkness: are those entities that serve the laws and tenets of the Dark Ways.

Lords of Law & Order: are those that serve the laws and tenants of the Light.

Love: is the highest expression of the Source in the universe. It can open greater more expanded awareness of life in individuals. In the Aquarian Age we are going to be looking at things through the glasses of love to transform and restore balance to all things in this world.

Lyrans: are one of the ancient extraterrestrial races. They appear like elves of legends when they appear to the younger species. They have been actively involved with Human Affairs for many millions of years.

ℳ

Magnetizing: is the meditation that attracts things to one's vibrational field.

Marriage: is one of the five social institutions of a society. In the age of Aquarius this institution is going to restore equality to all in a given Society.

Master: is the sixth stage of the level of psychic development. Individuals at this level have attained a certain degree of Mastery over their abilities through years of practice and experience.

Master's Degree: is part of the sixth level of Soul Development. Individual Souls at this level of development have been reincarnating for many lifetimes. They have learned who they are in regards to the larger community and will go to Great Lengths to serve their local and state regions.

Mediumship: is the fourth level of psychic development. Individuals with this gift can see and interact with entities from the higher dimensions. They can do this without having those entities entering into their physical form to communicate.

Melcheizeldek Order: are members of the elite forces of the Archangel Michael. They are the protectors and Guardians of the Council of light and Order.

Metaphysical: is anything that is part of the Unseen aspects of the universe. It is also part of esoteric teachings which have been handed down to those Seekers who are following a certain mystical path. In recent years quantum physics has started to grasp and explain some of the same knowledge that was expressed for Millennium by Mystics and avatars.

Milky Way Galaxy: is the Galaxy in which we are now residing.

Moral Compass: is the inner guidance all people have for determining what is right for them as individuals.

Morality: is an individual concept of what is right or wrong for their reality.

Mother Earth: is that feminine spirit that is representative of the living form of our planet.

Mountain Stance: is the yoga position that has you standing with your legs shoulder-width apart.

Mudras: are movements to express prayer. they were developed by the sufis thousands of years ago.

𝒩

Nanotechnology: is minuscule machines and computer parts.

Negativity: is the thoughts and attitudes that create problems in one's life.

New Age: in reference to this book, it is the Aquarian Age.

Nomadic: is part of the first level of Soul Development. Individuals at this level have not had very many lifetimes and they usually have a very fresh attitude towards life.

Novice: is the second stage of psychic development. Individuals at this stage are still learning to develop their abilities and will need aid from teachers to guide them in the appropriate use of their gifts.

NU: is one of the planetary systems of the Pleiades.

Numan: is the head of a household and planetary system of NU within the Pleiades system. Most of the archangels come from this system.

O

Orallens: are one of the Elder extraterrestrial races. They reside in the Orion's Belt planetary system. They were taken by the Sirians and the Pleiadians at the end of the Great Dragon War.

They serve the Lord's Order and Light.

Orange: is one of the secondary colors. It is associated with the second chakra just below the belly button. It is associated with creativity, abundance and sex.

Organic Technology: is technology that is organic in nature. Some of the technology is alive and has Consciousness. For the most part this technology Works within the confines of the natural world so as not interrupt the flow of energy in all things.

Orion's: see the Orallens and the Col'Notatros.

Osiris: is one of the heads of the House and planetary system of IS in the Pleiades.

Paradigm: is a pattern of reality. During the Aquarian Age are shifting at an alarming rate to restore the balance of this planet.

Past Lives: are those lifetimes an individual soul has lived.

Pathic Abilities: are those abilities of the Psychic Trinity that deal with interrelationship skills.

Personal Power Chakra: Is the individual chakra where the person holds their spiritual power. It is completely separate from the third chakra which is known as the power chakra.

Pituitary Gland: is the gland within the brain that monitors the balance within the body using endorphins. It is associated with the psychic abilities.

Piscean Age: is the period of time that was left in 1981.

Pisces: is one of the twelve Zodiac signs of Western astrology. It is associated with sacrifice, compassion, teachers, psychsim, the element of water and the planet Neptune.

Platonic: is the Christian theologian's concept of brotherly love.

Pleiadians: are one of the ancient extraterrestrial races. The planetary systems are associated with the Seven Heavens from early religious texts. They head up several groups within the Spiritual Hierarchy.

Power Chakra: is the third energy center along the spinal column. It is associated with the color yellow, and willpower. It is located between the navel and the diaphragm.

Precognition: allows the individual to see things before they happen it is associated with Seers, psychics and Visionaries.

Priest: is a male initiate of a deep spiritual and mystical background.

Priestess: is a female initiate of a deep spiritual and mystical background

Protestant: is an offshoot from the Catholic Church. Followers of this religious Faith develop their own dogmatic system loosely based on Christian beliefs.

Psychic: is the first level of psychic development. Individuals with this gift will be able to utilize any of the psychic aspects to help others on the journey.

Psychic Ability: is any of the gifts to see into the higher planes. It utilizes any of the psychic aspects and the levels of psychic development.

Psychic Aspects: are parts of the psychic Trinity. They are Clairvoyance, Clairaudience, Clair salience, Claircognizance, Clairsentience, Clairempathy, Clairtangience, and Clairgustance. They help you to see and know things clearly in the higher dimensions. These aspects usually go together with the other areas of the Psychic Trinity to make up the psychic gifts.

Psychic Development: is part of the Psychic Trinity. Individuals can develop their psychic abilities through practice and experience. Those abilities are Psychic, Seer, Channel, Mediumship, Visionary, Creator and Avatar. They are also tied in with the development of awareness within a soul.

Psychic Protection: is the ability to protect your energetic body from external psychic attack.

Psychic Trinity: is complete working units of psychic talents. These are the psychic aspects the levels of psychic development and the Pathic Abilities.

Psychic Vampires: are those individuals who have become so engrossed in the negative thinking that they thrive upon the suffering of others. They will drain innocent people of their psychic life Force if given a chance.

2

Quan Yin: is the Buddhist goddess of compassion and mercy. She is a manifestation of the feminine that is found in every culture across the planet.

R

Race: is related to different species from human origins. In recent centuries it has been inaccurately added to include people that look different from the majority group in control on the planet Earth.

RE: is the head of the house and planetary system of KERA within the Pleiades.

Receive: is the ability to be open to the information or gifts from the universe or others. In regards to the pathic abilities, it means to be open to the information being related to you.

Reception: see receive.

Recycle: is to use something again to prevent waste.

Red: is one of the primary colors. It is associated with survival issues, aggressive motivation and the base chakra.

Reincarnation: is the process whereby the individual soul incarnates into multiple lifetimes to work towards returning itself to the Source.

Religion: is one of the five social institutions. It is associated with passing on the template about the reason for the way things are in the universe. It provides the universal needs of a cultural identity to a group of people. In the Aquarian age religions are undergoing a major paradigm shift because the people of the planet are coming together as one world.

Right to Choose: in this sector of the Milky Way galaxy, this has been granted in order to see what will happen to a younger species. Due to this, individuals on this planet have the right to follow whatever path on which they feel most comfortable. The spiritual hierarchy has recently changed its attitude towards humans living on the planet Earth.

ſ

Sagittarius: is one of the twelve Zodiac signs of Western astrology. It is associated with freedom, change, philosophy, sportsmanship, the element of fire and the planet Mars.

Sananda: is one of the ascended masters that taught me during the Intergalactic classroom in my adolescence. He is one of the bearers of the cosmic consciousness. He is also the former head of the house and planetary system of AN in the Pleiades. He is also known as Jesus the Nazarene in one of his previous lifetimes.

SARAH: is the head of the house and planetary system of SERA in the Pleiades.

Scorpio: is one of the twelve Zodiac signs in Western astrology. It is associated with intensity, transformation, the planet Pluto and the element of water.

Seeing: is what a Seer or Visionary have during a trance.

Seer: is the second level of psychic development. Individuals at this level have visions of possible events relating to others in their environment. This ability is commonly associated with the psychic aspect of clairvoyance.

Send: in conjunction with the Pathic Abilities, it is the ability to project information and knowledge to others.

Sensitives: are an old reference to people with active psychic gifts.

SERA: is one of the houses and planetary systems within the Pleiades. They are commonly associated with Seraphim of the sixth heaven. They are often referred to as the "Voice of God". In the Pleiades they are one of the Protectors of the House of AN.

Seraphim: see SERA.

Seven Heavens: in ancient religious texts the heavens were divided into seven distinct areas as one got closer to the manifestation of God. In actuality it is related to the Pleiadian star system. Each of the seven planetary systems within the Pleiades is directly related to the seven heavens mentioned in these ancient texts. Those texts were left in the care of the priesthood of various cultures to deify the Pleiadian Masters.

Sex Chakra: is one of the seven energetic fields that lie along the spinal column. This field is the color orange and is frequently associated with sex and creativity. See Orange.

Sexless: is to be without gender.

Shields: are those barriers created to protect individuals from psychic or magical attacks.

Sight: is the ability to see things using clairvoyance.

Silver Cord: is the connection to your physical self while astral projecting.

SIrians: are one of the oldest of the ancient extraterrestrial races. They have been traveling the stars were several billions of years. There are very few of them left and they rarely interact with Humanity. They are from the Sirius Major (A and B) star system.

Sixth Sense: is often referred to as psychic ability. It is the latent aspect of our brain that will become active during the Aquarian Age.

Social Institutions: are those things within a society which helped to create and promote the social identity of a society.

Society: is a group of individuals who share common ideals values and beliefs.

Soul: see the divine spark.

Soul Development: is the path the individual soul takes over the course of many lifetimes.

Soul Family: is the group of individual Souls that began incarnating together over many lifetimes into family units.

Soul Group: is the group of souls that have been incarnating together over multiple lifetimes. These individuals may not be related in this lifetime. The connection and deep foundation of love that is present with these individuals creates a strong network for the present. In the Aquarian Age soul groups will help to stabilize the erosions of the family unit.

Sounds: are vibrations of frequency that can be utilized during meditation to acquire various states of awareness.

Source: is the origin of everything in the universe.

Spirit Guides: are those entities from the higher Dimensions who are here to assist and guide individuals on their journey through life. They are usually Angels or deceased relatives that are honoring the sacred contract.

Spirit Self: is the aspect of your soul that is allowed to journey in the astral planes.

Spiritual Hierarchy: is the 14 councils that guide and assist the youngest species in their evolutionary process. They also maintain the balance in the universe between Order and Chaos. See Chapter 4 for more details on the hierarchy.

Stages: are the subordinate areas of the levels of psychic development.

Status Quo: is how things are throughout a given period of time. It is believed by many that this never changes but it always has throughout human history.

Stressor: is anything that might contribute to stress in one's life.

𝒯

Taurus: is one of the 12 Zodiac signs of Western astrology. It is associated with earthiness, steadfastness, the spring, the element of earth, and the planet Venus.

Technocracy: is a government based on science and technology. It is usually headed by the chief scientist of a society.

Teenager: is part of the fourth level of Soul development. People at this level often have been reincarnating for a long time. They learn to explore more of who they are as individuals of spiritually and mentally.

Telepathy: is one of the Pathic abilities. It allows individuals to communicate mind-to-mind without the use of vocal cords.

"Thank You" List: is a list designed to create a feeling of gratitude.

Third Eye Chakra: is one of the seven energetic centers along the spinal column. It actually is on the temple right above the brow. It is closely tied to the pineal gland. It is also associated with the colors Indigo and it promotes psychic experience and spiritual visions. It promotes psychic experiences when open.

Throat Chakra: is one of the seven energetic centers along the spinal column. It is located at the indention on the top of the sternum. It is associated with communication in all its forms and the color blue.

Town: is the fourth level of soul development see teenager for more details.

Toxic Person: is an individual who has built so much negative energy that they adversely affect the reality around them.

Transition Period: Is the period of time between the ages. It is usually 50 years on either side of a specific date of change into a new age. It is marked by dramatic events on the social and physical levels.

Tribal: is the second level of soul development. Individuals have only been incarnating for about 50 lifetimes and are just beginning to explore the larger reality through new interactions with others. This level is marked by tribes or gangs of people uniting together for common survival issues.

Transcendental Train Ride: is the meditation that allows you the individual to explore their past lives.

U

Universal Laws: are those laws which govern the basic nature of the universe.

Universal Needs: are those things that are needed by every society in order to create a unified cultural identity.

V

Vibration: the frequency which everything in this universe flows.

Vibrational Energy: see vibration.

Village: is the third level of soul development. These are middle-aged Souls that are more concerned with fitting into the larger community than actually learning who they are as individuals.

Violet: is one of the secondary colors. It is associated with divinity and direct connection to the source. It is also related to the crown chakra.

Virgo: is one of the 12 signs of western astrology. It is associated with the vestal virgins of early goddess worship, health, perfection, the element of earth, and the planet Mercury.

Visionary: is the fifth level of psychic development. Individuals at this level will have visions that pertain to the larger world.

Visualization: is the concept of imagining in your mind's eye what it is you wish to create.

Y

Yellow: is one of the primary colors. It is associated with happiness, positive energy, will power, and the third chakra.

Z

Zeta Reticulans: are one of the elder extraterrestrial races. They are the most commonly known extraterrestrial to the human race in modern times. They are also known as the "Grays." Due to their inability to breed they have been performing experiments on humanity for more than millenia.

.

Printed in the United States
By Bookmasters